AMERICAN SCHOOL OF PREHISTORIC RESEARCH

PEABODY MUSEUM, HARVARD UNIVERSITY

BULLETIN 25

MECKLENBURG COLLECTION, PART I

DATA ON IRON AGE HORSES OF CENTRAL AND EASTERN EUROPE

BY

SÁNDOR BÖKÖNYI

AND

HUMAN SKELETAL MATERIAL FROM SLOVENIA

BY

J. LAWRENCE ANGEL

Edited by HUGH HENCKEN

CAMBRIDGE, MASSACHUSETTS, U.S.A.
PUBLISHED BY THE PEABODY MUSEUM
1968

© Copyright 1968 by the President
and Fellows of Harvard College

Library of Congress Catalog Card Number 68-22588

PRINTED BY THE CRIMSON PRINTING COMPANY
CAMBRIDGE, MASSACHUSETTS, U.S.A.

BOUND BY STANHOPE BINDERY, INCORPORATED
BOSTON, MASSACHUSETTS

CONTENTS

DATA ON IRON AGE HORSES OF CENTRAL AND EASTERN EUROPE (SÁNDOR BÖKÖNYI)

LIST OF ILLUSTRATIONS

HUMAN SKELETAL MATERIAL FROM SLOVENIA (J. L. ANGEL)

LIST OF ILLUSTRATIONS

INTRODUCTION

THIS is the first of a series of volumes dealing with the Mecklenburg Collection and in consequence something must be said about the history of this great assemblage of Iron Age material. The scene of the greater part of the work was the former Austrian province of Krain or Carniola, now included in the Slovene Republic, the westernmost part of Jugoslavia.

The excavator was the Duchess Paul Friedrich von Mecklenburg-Schwerin. She was born Princess Marie von Windischgrätz, and was thus a member of an Austrian family with estates in Carniola. Her own home was Schloss Wagensberg, now Bogenšperk, near Litija some 30 km. east of Ljubljana. She carried out very extensive excavations in what is now Slovenia at Magdalenska gora, Vinica, the vicinity of Stična and a number of other localities, and also at the great cemetery of Hallstatt in Upper Austria. Her work began in 1905 and continued until August 2, 1914 and the outbreak of the First World War. Kaiser Wilhelm II, himself a keen amateur archaeologist, was greatly interested in her excavations and on two occasions in 1913 and early 1914 sent her subventions of 100,000 marks each.

The Duchess was also well acquainted with two of the greatest prehistorians of the day, Oscar Montelius and Joseph Déchelette, both of whom visited her excavations. She also made a practice, not always followed at that time, of keeping separate the entire contents of each grave. Montelius in a letter advised her to make plans and sections of the very large tumuli that she excavated, but unfortunately no such drawings have survived.

The Duchess kept the greater part of her material except for a cuirass from Šentvid (St. Veit) near Stična and some helmets and a few other objects which she sent to Kaiser Wilhelm. I am grateful to Mr. Gustaf Mahr for his efforts to locate these objects in Berlin. On the death of the Duchess Paul Friedrich the collection was inherited by her daughter, the Duchess Marie Antoinette, but at the end of the First World War it was confiscated and was taken to the National Museum of Slovenia at Ljubljana. In 1929 title to it was returned to the Duchess Marie Antoinette, and she obtained the permission of the late King Alexander of Jugoslavia to sell it abroad. It was sent to Zurich, but some objects, at the invitation of the Duchess, were retained by the National Museum at Ljubljana.[1]

The National Museum has been extremely cooperative in supplying information about this material and illustrations of it for inclusion with the relevant grave groups to be published in this series.

The objects sent to Zurich, comprising by far the larger part of the collection, were entrusted for sale to the American Art Association Anderson Galleries of New York. To catalogue the collection this firm engaged the services of the late Dr. Adolf Mahr of the National Museum, Dublin and formerly of the Naturhistorisches Museum, Vienna. He in turn assembled the following group of distinguished prehistorians to assist him:

Dr. Georg Bierbaum, Dresden
Dr. Sándor Gallus, Sopron
Dr. Friedrich Holste, Marburg a.d. Lahn
Professor Raymond Lantier, St.-Germain-en-Laye
Professor Gero von Merhart, Marburg a.d. Lahn
Mr. J. M. de Navarro, Cambridge
Professor Balduin Saria, Ljubljana
Dr. Ferenc de Tompa, Budapest
Professor Emil Vogt, Zurich

These archaeologists prepared a massive card index of the whole material, 996 graves plus a considerable quantity of other objects that could be attributed to a specific tumulus or to a cemetery but not to an individual grave. The cards for each grave give the cemetery, the tumulus, such documentation as was available, a list of the objects and photographs of most of them. This index served as the basis for the

---

[1] Rajko Ložar, Predzgodovina Slovenije, posebej Kranjske, v luči zbirke Mecklenburg, *Glasnik muzejskega društva za Slovenijo*, vol. 15, 1934, pp. 5–91.

sale catalogue, *Treasures of Carniola*, issued by the American Art Association Anderson Galleries in 1934.

The expected sale, however, did not take place. The Peabody Museum of Harvard University, in order to prevent the dispersal of the collection with the attendant loss to science, made great efforts to see that it was divided among major museums. Response to these efforts was meager, and in 1934 the Peabody Museum purchased the first 48 lots comprising the material from Magdalenska gora. Soon thereafter the Ashmolean Museum at Oxford purchased Lots 140 to 147, the material from Vače or Watsch. In 1940 the Peabody Museum acquired all the rest of the collection. During the long intervening period since our purchases, the objects have been as far as possible cleaned, restored, and drawn for publication.

The next question is to what extent can one trust the grave groups as they came to us. This situation is of course not perfect. Not all the objects from every grave could be found by the cataloguers in Zurich, and occasionally an entire grave is missing. Also there are some cases in which sherds of the same pot or bones of the same skeleton were attributed to more than one grave. We cannot of course now tell whether this was due to the inevitable confusion resulting from many graves being dug into the same tumulus, or whether some objects may have been misplaced during or after the excavations. Nonetheless it was the opinion of Dr. Mahr and those who organized the card index that enough reliable information was available to make the collection of scientific importance. This view was expressed to me especially by Mahr, Merhart and de Navarro. In any case, little further confusion has occurred since the card index was made. This card index, except the part dealing with Vače, came to us with the collection, and with a few trivial exceptions the objects in the grave groups at the Peabody Museum correspond to those indexed by Mahr and his associates.

Since the collection has been unavailable for so long to scholars, it is my intention to publish the material grave by grave in a series of volumes, according to Mahr's card index, leaving extended discussion until later.

It happens that the reports on the bones of the horses by Dr. S. Bökönyi of the Magyar Nemzeti Muzeum, Budapest, and on the human remains by Dr. J. Lawrence Angel of the Smithsonian Institution, Washington, D.C. have been completed first. These two studies might normally have been published as appendices, but under the circumstances it seems unreasonable to delay them.

I am deeply indebted to these two distinguished scholars for their invaluable co-operation in preparing these reports on essential parts of the study of the Mecklenburg Collection.

HUGH HENCKEN

GEOGRAPHICAL NAMES IN SLOVENIA
WITH ALTERNATE FORMS

Several of the alternative forms are those given by Adolf Mahr and others in the sale catalogue called *Treasures of Carniola* (Anderson Galleries, New York 1934). Some of these are incorrect, but they are given here anyway in order to make an equation with that catalogue possible. Dr. Stane Gabrovec of the National Museum, Ljubljana has been of very great assistance in dealing with these names and in placing them on the accompanying map.

Bela cerkev   (Weisskirchen)

Bogenšperk   (Wagensburg)

Dolenje Ležeče   (Lesece)

Družinska vas   (Gesindedorf)

Glogovica   (Vas Glogovica)

Lepence   (Lepinca)

Magdalenska gora   (Magdalenaberg or Magdalenenberg)

Nova mesto   (Rudolfswerth)

Nova vas   (see Višnja gora)

Pece   (Vas Pece)

Predjama   (Luegg)

Retje   (Retize)

Šentvid   (St. Veit)

Škocjan   (St. Canzian)

Šmarjeta   (St. Margarethen)

Šmihel   (St. Michael bei Luegg)

Socerb   (San Servolo)

Stična   (Sittich)

Vače   (Watsch)

Vinica   (Weinitz)

Vir   (Vas Vir)

Višnja gora   Here there is some confusion in *Treasures of Carniola*, p. 128. This mentions Neudorf near Mariathal (Dole), but there is no such place. The reference is probably to *Nova vas* (Neudorf) near Višnja gora, a well-known archaeological locality.

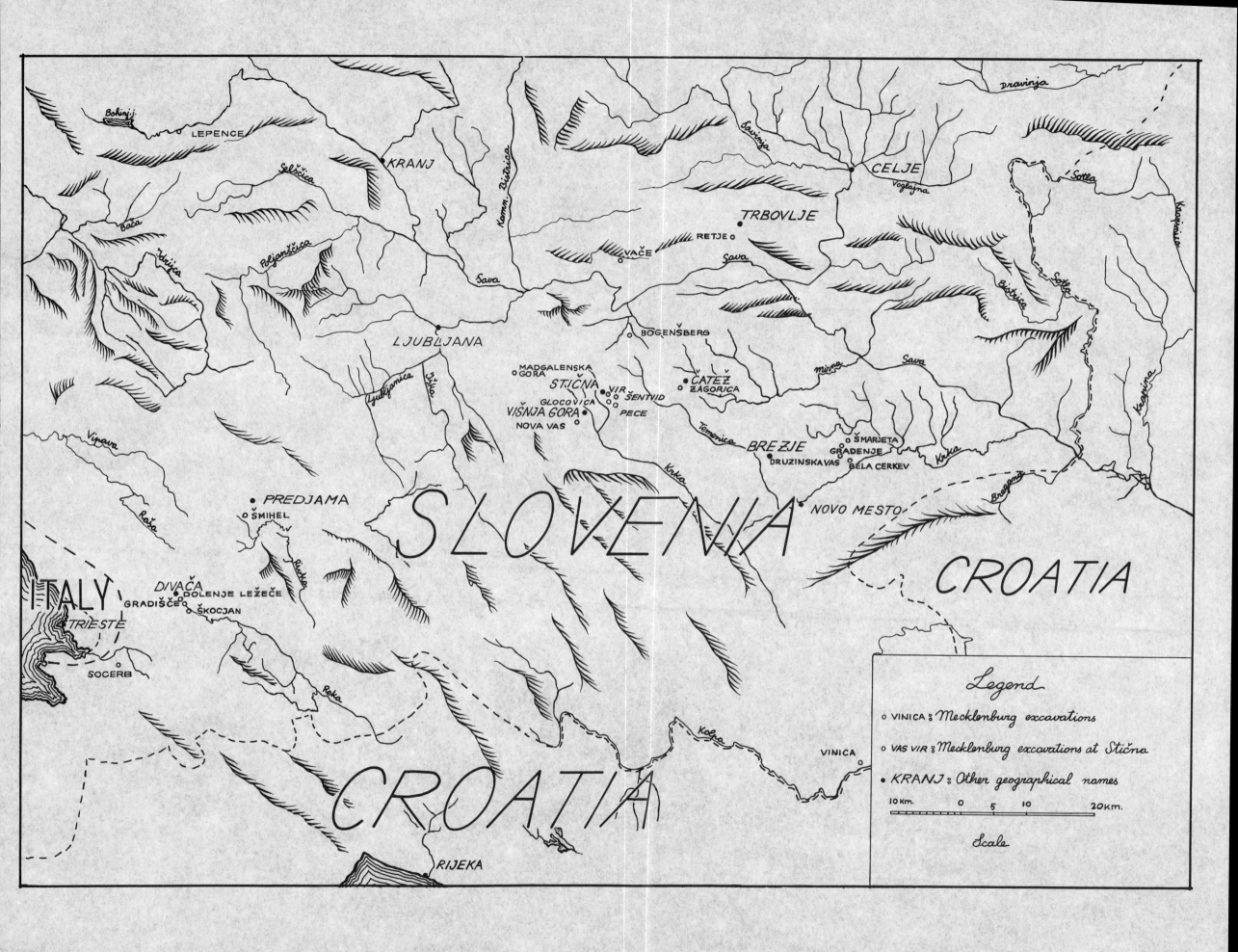

Legend

o VINICA ⸝ Mecklenburg excavations

o VAS VIR ⸝ Mecklenburg excavations at Stična

● KRANJ ⸝ Other geographical names

10 Km. 0 5 10   20 Km.

Scale

DATA ON IRON AGE HORSES OF CENTRAL AND EASTERN EUROPE

BY SÁNDOR BÖKÖNYI

DATA ON IRON AGE HORSES OF CENTRAL AND EASTERN EUROPE

FOREWORD

THE PROBLEM of a more thorough comparison of the Iron Age horses of Central and Eastern Europe arose while elaborating the horses of the Scythian cemetery at Szentes-Vekerzug, in the course of which we investigated how far west the type of Scythian horses found there had extended. For want of suitable published material we could not achieve any essential results at that time; we could only state that the Swiss Celtic horses described by Marek had been definitely differentiated from Scythian horses on a craniological basis. The essential difference is that while the facial part of the skull is short in the former, it is long in the latter, and if we consider the cerebral part of the skull of the two groups of equal length, the facial part of the Swiss Celtic horses is approximately one-third longer.

My talks with Prof. G. Kossack of the Institut für Ur- und Frühgeschichte, Kiel, further encouraged me to continue my investigations. On grounds of archaeological considerations Prof. Kossack expounded his conviction that the Celtic and Scythian horses must represent two different types and encouraged me to demonstrate this on an osteological basis.

The third incentive to direct my attention to these investigations emerged while the horses of the Hallstatt Age of Magdalenska gora and Šentvid in Slovenia were elaborated. Their detailed analysis pointed to the fact that these horses must be related to the Scythian horses of Szentes-Vekerzug. This relationship referred to sizes of bodies, proportions of bodies, certain characteristics of the skull—as will be seen from the following there are no intact skulls in the above material, only parts of the skulls— dental enamel pattern, the size of certain long bones as well as to their length and breadth relationship. All this means that the nomadic Scythians coming from the south of Russia to Central Europe had characteristic graves with horses, and these horses found in the latter region at Szentes-Vekerzug were the same horses as those possessed by certain local peoples who lived in the region at that time. In this connection the question arose whether it is not possible that in Central and Southeastern Europe there lived only a single but highly variable group of horses, and whether the Celtic and Scythian horses formerly considered so very different are not the extreme forms of this one type–two extreme forms which by the increasing material of the past years have now been connected by numerous transitional forms.

For this reason it was really on grounds of the material of Magdalenska gora and Šentvid that we decided to explore the question thoroughly. Lately we have been fortunate enough to get to know, mostly by autopsy, a great part of the subfossil horse finds of Central and Eastern Europe. In the course of our study, our tours have covered nine countries, Denmark, West Germany, Austria, Czechoslovakia, Poland, Hungary, the Soviet Union, Jugoslavia and Bulgaria. Although we have not been able to examine each horse find of the countries in question, we could get a picture of the material, which we could compare with the data of literature at our disposal and the dimensions and representations our colleagues were kind enough to make available for us. Thus we have been able to extend our investigations to so much material as, with respect to magnitude, has never been at the disposal of any researcher. We could draw our conclusions from the investigation of horse bone material representing more than 500 individuals.

Personal acknowledgments begin with an expression of gratitude to Dr. H. Hencken, Peabody Museum of Harvard University, Cambridge, USA, for allowing me to investigate the Hallstatt Age horse remains of Magdalenska gora and Šentvid and to Doc. Dr. K. Kromer, Naturhistorisches Museum, Wien, Austria, for those of Brezje; to Doc. Dr. J. Boessneck, Tieranatomisches Institut, München, German Federal Republic; to Mrs. A.

Paul-Bolomey, Institutul Arheologii, Bucuresti, Rumania, and to Prof. W. I. Zalkin, Moscow, Soviet Union, for submitting to me measurements of bones; to Mrs. A. P. Mantsevitch, Hermitage, Leningrad, Soviet Union, for sending me photographs of Scythian horse-representations; to Dr. I. Erdélyi, Research Group of Archaeology of the Hungarian Academy of Sciences, Budapest, Hungary and to Dr. M. Gábori, Municipal Museum, Budapest, Hungary, for putting at my disposal photographs of recent Mongolian horses.

CHAPTER I

HISTORY OF THE RESEARCH OF THE ORIGIN AND CLASSIFICATION OF DOMESTIC HORSES

THE APPEARANCE in the middle of the nineteenth century of the Dane Steenstrup and of the Swiss Rütimeyer indicate the beginning of research in the history of domestic animals. No less a personality than Charles Darwin was among the first to pursue these investigations. With respect to its development the research work can be divided into three phases. The first, essentially lasting from the beginning up to the First World War, was characterized by the researchers having examined small numbers of materials, and moreover the determination of the archaeological ages of these scanty materials was rather unstable, but, on the grounds of the small material enormous theories were set up regarding the origin, the routes of migration, and the history of domestic animals. Based on the investigations of this phase—which was pursued by researchers who having been active as palaeontologists or scientists of stockbreeding, subsequently took up this branch of research—the assumed ancestors of our domestic animals sprang up like mushrooms in the literature. So did the types and breeds of prehistoric domestic animals, and so did the assumed relations of origin between types of domestic animals found in prehistoric archaeological sites in Europe and of wild animals of remote areas, possibly of other continents. The second phase began in the twenties, after the First World War, and lasted until the Second. This phase was introduced by the comprehensive works of the Austrian Antonius and the German Hilzheimer in which the authors summarized the results of previous research and tried, first of all by means of abridgements and simplifications, to tidy up the confusion that had been created by the end of the previous period. Further research mostly proceeded from the grounds clarified by them and was characterized by the fact that side by side with the investigations of the science of breeds, on which the Schmidt-

Koppers school of ethnography had had a considerable influence, the investigations of faunistics were growing increasingly important, particularly in the second part of the phase. In the latter branch of research work Swiss authors were especially eminent. After the Second World War, in the late forties, when scientific life was resumed, the third phase began, which—according to the experience we have gained so far—is characterized by the following features:

1. Further simplifications, by the assumption of a monophyletic origin for essentially all species of domestic animals and by the contraction of breeds and types.

2. By a recession of the investigation of breeds based on craniology.

3. By examinations of faunistics and of variations of size carried out on a big material.

4. By a closer cooperation with archaeology and other branches of science, which made a more accurate determination of the time and place of the earliest domestication of different species of domestic animals possible.

5. By the introduction of new methods of examination.

We have mentioned all this because, knowing it, we can better follow and understand the course of investigations regarding the history of the domestic horse. Since, perhaps up to the most recent time, the horse was the domestic animal connected most closely to man, its history was most closely linked with man's history. Accordingly, a great many people dealt with the questions of its domestication and of its wild ancestors and the latter's classification into types. The theories which have been and are being created in connection with the above questions are extraordinarily varied and can be basically divided into six great groups:

1. Sanson, and Piètrement after him, divided the domestic horse into eight types, which ensues from what we mentioned above on the first phase of investigations on the history of domestic animals. Each

of these types was derived from different species of wild horses.

2. By the Czekanowski method based on the build of the skull and used by some authors in anthropology, Skorkowski divided domestic horses into six groups, assuming a separate wild ancestor for each of these groups.

3. Stegmann classified domestic horses into five groups, which he traced back to five wild types. Three of Stegmann's groups correspond, in essence, to the three types of Ewart (see next paragraph), while the fourth is nothing else than the desert horse of Duerst (see next paragraph), the fifth being a local steppe group originating from Central Asia.

4. Ewart divided horses into three groups, each with a separate wild ancestor: a) the steppe variety, their ancestor being the wild horse of Przewalski *(Equus przewalskii* Polj.); b) the forest variety, their ancestor being the wild horse of Solutré; c) the plateau variety, whose basic type is the so-called Celtic pony derived by Ewart from English fossil horses. Essentially, the same theory was professed by Brinkmann as well as by Duerst. The latter called the third Ewart type the desert horse and not the plateau variety. Similarly, Antonius denominated the three types as *Equus orientalis*, the wild ancestor being the Tarpan *(Equus gmelini* Ant.); *Equus ferus*, the wild ancestor being the Przewalski horse; and *Equus robustus*, the wild ancestor being the large-bodied diluvial horse of Western Europe. Hilzheimer gave the three groups the names of Tarpan group, Celtic Ponies and cold-blooded horse.

5. As against the above-mentioned researchers, Franck, Forsyth-Major, Nehring and Wilckens classified the domestic horse into two groups: an occidental (cold-blooded) and an oriental (warm-blooded) group and derived them from separate wild ancestors. The occidental group corresponds with Ewart's forest variety and the oriental with Ewart's steppe variety. This grouping based on Franck's investigations on molars has become very widespread and practical stockbreeders classify horses on this basis even today. Regarding the wild ancestors, essentially the same view has been adopted by Lundholm too, who, with respect to domestication, acknowledges two types of wild horses that can be taken into consideration, but Ebhardt is also an adherent of the diphyletic theory and divides domestic horses into two groups, "ponies" and "horses," and within this grouping again into two subgroups.

6. Finally, we mention the monophyletic theory which assumes one wild ancestor. Darwin was the first to put forward this theory. Much later Schwartz's investigations gave a further impetus to the development of this theory, which has recently been most vigorously represented by Herre and his school. In the European Mesolithic and Neolithic Ages—according to this theory—there existed only one species of wild horses, which, in all likelihood, was identical with the Przewalski horse and all former and present domestic horses can be traced back to this species.

It is evident from the above that the theory of the origin and grouping of the domestic horse has come a long and varied way from the eight types and wild ancestors respectively put forward by Sanson to the only wild ancestor assumed by the monophyletic theory. In essential points it has covered all the above outlined phases of the history of domestic animals. The aforementioned process of simplification is clearly manifested in this question too. However, we do not know whether the grade of simplification represented by the monophyletic theory is not exaggerated, since, when the theory was built up, the immense material of wild horses' bones of the eastern part of Central Europe, of Eastern Europe and of Central Asia had not been taken into consideration. The elaboration of this material has so far only been carried out partly, whereas its comprehensive discussion will only be forthcoming in the future.

The earliest domestication of the horse could only take place toward the end of the Neolithic Age or in the Copper Age respectively, most probably in several places simultaneously. We do not wish to deal with the fantastic theories of old authors; we only outline the concept of more recent ones. Of the latter, Gandert presumes two centers of domestication, the central part of Europe and Central Asia, and Vogel (1933), three, Central Asia, the south of Russia and the northwest of Germany; according to Lundholm there were domestication centers on the coast of the North Sea, in the British Isles, in Spain and on the coast of the Black Sea. According to Hančar the first domestication of the horse took place in Qalat Jarmo, about 4500 B.C., while in Europe domestication began in the middle of the third millennium in the following territories: in the north of Europe and the woodland and steppe region of the Upper Dniester, the area of the Tripolje Culture. According to Hančar domestication took place at the same time in the steppe region of Siberia, too, the region of the Afanasyevo Culture. Against them, Herre (1958) assumes a single domestication center to have existed in Europe, in fact in Central Europe. On the other hand, Huppertz (1961) presumes that the earliest domestication of the horse took place in the Turanian-Altaic region. In our opinion, it seems in any case probable that the earliest and most significant domestication center of the horse must have been on the steppes of Asia or Eastern Europe for it was only there that a substantial material of wild horses, which had survived the Pleistocene Age, was found from the Neolithic Age. From there the first domestic horses got to Europe, where as a result domestication also started. However, here—at least in the greater part of Central Europe—domestication never reached a serious level, and it was always the horses introduced from the East that were prevailing.

Even if the question of the time and place of the earliest domestication is open to debate, the fact that the horse became a significant domestic animal in Europe at the very beginning of the Bronze Age has been well known for long (Hescheler, 1929–30; 1933; Degerböl, 1935; Hermes, 1936; Vogel, 1940; Hescheler–Kuhn, 1949; La Baume, 1953; Nobis, 1957; Herre, 1958; Lepiksaar. 1962; etc.). This indicates that sporadically it must have been found here already in the course of the Copper Age, as is assumed by numerous authors (Hilzheimer, 1935; Banner, 1939; Lundholm, 1947; Bökönyi, 1954; Hančar, 1956; Boessneck, 1958; Skorkowski, 1958; etc.). Since there are no essential anatomical differences between the bones of domestic and of wild horses, a most convenient standpoint has recently been taken up by the historians of domestic animals all over Europe —and this standpoint is due to the fact that the domestic horse spread very quickly during the Bronze Age—i.e., to derive all horse finds of the Bronze Age or of a later date from the domestic horse and those from ages prior to the Bronze Age from the wild horse. It is, at most, with finds from the late Neolithic–Copper Age

that some of them will make exceptions. In fact, it is difficult to prove that there were domestic horses to be found prior to the Bronze Age. Even if we try to draw conclusions from finds of bridles—as Hermes (1935) did, "Wo die Trense, dort ist in der Regel auch das gezähmte Pferd..."—this does not help a lot in proving that domestic horses were to be met, since the earliest bridles made of bones or antlers date back to the middle of the Bronze Age (Mozsolics, 1953) when domestic horses had existed for long. The application of the bridle seems to be connected with the use of the horse as a riding animal; earlier, when horses were only used as draught animals, no bridles were used, only muzzle straps. Artsikhovsky's method (1947) for determining whether the horse bones of a site originated from a population of domestic or wild horses is a very interesting one. According to this method, if the finds of the horse bones of a settlement contain complete skeletons, if there are no old animals among them and if the number of females is prevalent, this points to a domesticated population, whereas the lack of vertebrae and of sterna, the occurrence of very old animals and an equal number of males and females points to a wild population. Unfortunately, the practical application of this method is rendered impossible by the circumstance that in the European Neolithic sites in question there are only one or two horse bones to be found as a rule and this material is absolutely unsuitable for the purposes of a statistical investigation. It would be worthwhile to study more thoroughly the separation of the bones of domesticated and of wild horses, perhaps with the application of investigation methods not used up to now (Roentgen analysis). In our view the most expedient way would be to approach the question from several sides at the same time and to develop some complex method.

Chapter II

EUROPEAN DOMESTIC HORSES OF THE PREHISTORIC AGE

NEARLY all former authors used to range European domestic horses of the Prehistoric Age with the oriental race group, since on grounds of the diphyletic theory, which had become highly popular, they considered all small-bodied horses to be of oriental origin.

Thus Studer (1900) considered the horses of Swiss pile dwellings of the Bronze Age as belonging to the oriental race. So did Marek (1898) and Schwertz (1918) with respect to the La Tène horses, Naumann (1875) to the horses of pile dwellings on the Starnberger See, Hescheler (1933) to the horses of the Bronze Age of Switzerland, Riedel (1951) to the horses of the Italian sites of the Bronze Age, Amschler (1949) to the horses of the late Copper Age and the Iron Age in Austria, etc. However, since it has turned out that the large-bodied occidental horses only developed at the time of the post-Roman migration period (Nobis, 1955) and in the Middle Ages respectively (Boessneck, 1958), the oriental origin of the horses of the Prehistoric Age in Central and Western Europe has hardly been mentioned recently. Recent authors mostly derive them from local wild horses. It should be pointed out at this instance that Lundholm had assumed some connections to have existed between European domestic horses of prehistoric times and local wild horses.

Knowing the routes of migration and the identity of horses of East and Southeast Europe of the same period, it was much more justified than the above assumptions to consider the Bronze Age and Scythian horses of Hungary to be of oriental origin (Bökönyi, 1952; 1954; 1955). Although we know very little about the prehistoric domestic horse of Southeast Europe we may rightly assume its oriental origin, the more so as the number of wild horses which could serve as a basis for domestication were to be found there in the alluvium only in small numbers, nor did considerable western elements find their way there in the course of the Prehistoric Age. From Eastern Europe we know mostly about the horses of the Tripolje Culture, described by Gromova as small-bodied, big-headed horses. On grounds of the material of the later periods of the Tripolje Culture found recently, it seems to be highly probable that a very early center of horse domestication existed in the Ukraine (Bibikova, 1962).

When summarizing the data gathered so far regarding the European domestic horse of the Iron Age, Marek's examinations carried out on the Swiss horses of the La Tène Period, as he calls them, the "Helvetian-Gallic" horses, are to be mentioned first. As a result of his investigations he stated that these horses belonged to the oriental race group and resemble—except in the sizes of their bodies—the Arab horse, the typical representative of the oriental group. According to Marek the identity with the members of the oriental race group can be ascertained from the skull (with the exception of one horse which he considered a cross-breed of the oriental and occidental types) as well as from the bones of the extremities. The same conformity with the Swiss horse of the Bronze Age can also be observed. Marek supposes the withers height of the "Helvetian-Gallic" horse to have been 135.5–141 cm.

Schwertz similarly considers the La Tène horses to be of oriental origin and bases this statement, like Marek, first of all upon the breadth of the front.

The only horse bone found at the Hallstatt Age settlement at Sissacherfluh near Basel is considered by Leuthardt as originating from a small-bodied animal but he does not indicate the origin in further particulars.

The vast material of horse bones of the Celtic *oppidum* excavated near Manching, about 13,000 bones, was elaborated by Liepe, Förster and Frank. Förster only carried out examinations on the phalanges, so we shall not deal with them but only with the results achieved by the other two authors. The investigations of Liepe and Frank carried out on the material of two different excavation periods of the site have brought almost exactly similar results. They have stated that, with the exception of a few pieces, the horse bones found at Manching originate from small-bodied and fine-boned horses of the oriental type, whose withers height was between 112 and 137 cm. Both authors identified the breed found at Manching first of all with the Bronze Age–La Tène Age horses of Switzerland, Bohemia and Moravia but stated that the size of its body is somewhat smaller than that of the latter and that the measurements of the smallest individuals hardly surpass those of asses. Besides this group, and not too much separated from it, there occurred some large-bodied individuals among which the withers height of the largest is above 150 cm. According to Liepe these may originate from Roman imports and this assumption is accepted by Frank too; he, however, adds that they might be gelded animals.

As we have seen above, there are data at our disposal regarding Scythian horses from the eastern part of Central Europe. These data were obtained from the examination of the horse skeletons found at the Scythian cemetery of Szentes-Vekerzug (Bökönyi, 1952; 1954; 1955). These horses were small of body, slender of legs and fine of constitution and can be ranged with the oriental group; genetically they can be related to the wild horse of Southern Russia, the tarpan, irrespective of whether we accept the wild character of the tarpan or not (Gromova, 1959; Herre, 1939; Nobis, 1955; Skorkowski, 1938). On grounds of their short facial and nasal part they can be separated well from the Celtic horses of Marek and can be considered as identical with the East European Scythian horses.

Ivanov and Markov described Thracian horses from the Iron Age of Southeast Europe. Both of the authors consider these animals to be thin-legged, slender-bodied animals belonging to the oriental breed.

Bibikova (1958) and Zalkin (1960) dealt with remains of horses from the southern part of eastern Europe from the same period. The former described horses as well as asses and even mules from Olbia, the colonial town of the Greeks on the northern shore of the Black Sea, whereas the latter examined the horse bone material unearthed in the course of exca-

vations of the Scythian and Greek settlements on the northern coastal area of the Black Sea. The results of both are fairly similar, which is not surprising if we consider first of all the trade connections that existed between the inhabitants of the above-mentioned Greek colonial town and the Scythians who lived on the steppes near by. Zalkin, by the way, found a single but highly variable type of horse on the sites of the Iron Age in the Black Sea region, both in Scythian settlements and in Greek colonial towns. The dwarfish individuals of this type, which are very rare, make up only 1.7 per cent of the total material and have a withers height of 120–128 cm., whereas the giant individuals, also very rare, amounting only to 1.2 per cent of the total, have a withers height of 152–160 cm. It is interesting that, according to the author, big-bodied horses of Asian origin of the period are not to be found on these sites, which in the author's opinion is due to the fact that he has elaborated the material of settlements, whereas the big-bodied "luxury-horses" imported from Asia should be looked for in the "kurgans," the burial places of people of distinction.

Since the Scythian horses of Eastern Europe are connected with those of Central Asia with a thousand links, we think we had better deal in short with the Central Asian horses of the Iron Age, too, the more so as—owing to lucky finds—here we may obtain data which are not available from the investigations of European horses of the Iron Age. Vitt and Zalkin (1952) have dealt with the horse remains of the Scythian kurgans of Central Asia. Vitt's paper gives a particularly detailed study of the Central Asian horse material of the Iron Age; the work being a summary of the investigations the author pursued for twenty years regarding the horse burials of the Altaian kurgans. Vitt's investigations cover the horses of the kurgans of Pazyryk and that of Sibe. As, due to special geological and climatic circumstances, the horses buried there had got mummified, the author was in the lucky position that he could examine not only the bones but could also collect data with respect to the color, the quality of the hair, the condition, the trappings, etc. of the horses as well. No other researcher had been in a position to do so. In each kurgan at Pazyryk there were 7–14 horses buried, while in the Sibe kurgan there were 14. Vitt stated that in the kurgans the corpses of horses were placed in rows and in each kurgan the first horse laid in the row was a big-bodied animal in good condition, with rich trappings and a mask on its face. In the author's opinion this horse did not necessarily belong to another breed than the rest of the horses in the kurgan but had grown bigger only owing to better feeding or else to gelding. In other places, however, Vitt refers to these horses originating from a breed different from that of the others. On grounds of the basal length of the skull Vitt classified these horses as belonging to four groups, which, however, were of the same race. The average withers height of these groups is 132, 136, 140 and 145 cm. The masked horses, which obviously were the favorite mounts of the distinguished personage buried in the kurgan, belonged to this last group of largest horses. The horses were of different shades of yellow, there were no white spots on them at all and their manes were mostly cut short. Uneven wrinkles are to be found on the horny surfaces of some horses' hooves, which testify to the starvation the animals had to suffer in the course of long winters. No such wrinkles are to be seen on the hooves of the masked horses, which, in addition to their good condition, also proves that they were better fed. Essentially Zalkin found horses similar to those described by Vitt, although the former marked out two definite groups, that of the average

"steppe" horses, which corresponds with the bulk of the Vitt horses, and that of large-bodied horses, which can be identified with the masked horses of Vitt. In one striking feature all of the skeletons examined by Zalkin tally: on all of them pathological lesions suggesting lameness could be observed. This means that it was not the good horses that were placed in the tombs but those already worn out. With respect to withers height the horses examined by Zalkin showed almost exactly the same picture as those investigated by Vitt, their withers heights being between 128.5 and 148 cm.

It is evinced by the foregoing that so far no clear picture has been formed in literature regarding European horses of the Prehistoric Age or their grouping. In addition to the incompleteness of the material, it may be enough to consider at this instance that the horses of the Iron Age found on about 40 sites in the vast territory stretching from the Alps to the Altai Mountains have been elaborated by only 11 authors altogether, which is next to nothing. This is, first of all, due to the fact that the material at their disposal has been examined by authors from most different points of view and with widely differing methods of measurements. Moreover, in most cases they examined a material slight in amount, which they discussed mostly in an isolated way and did not compare with the material found on other sites.

CHAPTER III

CHAPTER III

THE MATERIAL ELABORATED IN THE PRESENT WORK

AS MENTIONED in the foreword, in recent years we have had the opportunity to go on study tours in nearly all countries of Central and Eastern Europe in order to survey the subfossil horse finds unearthed there. A considerable part of the material we have examined has already been published. In such cases we only surveyed the material and completed certain measurements for, as already mentioned, the different authors employed the most diverse methods of measurements, whereas in a large, comprehensive work it is indispensable that the whole material should be measured on grounds of identical principles of measurement and possibly measured by the same hands. Another part of the material is now being published for the first time. The horses of the Hallstatt Age of Magdalenska gora and the cemetery of Šentvid at Stična belong to the latter group (Peabody Museum of Harvard University, Cambridge, USA), offered by Dr. H. Hencken for elaboration; the horses of the Hallstatt Age of Brezje in Krain (Naturhistorisches Museum, Wien, Austria); the material of Dr. K. Kromer, and from the archaeological sites of the Hallstatt Age in Hungary, horse bones from the Scythian cemetery at Tápioszele (Magyar Nemzeti Muzeum —Hungarian National Museum, Budapest); from the earlier excavations of the Szentes-Vekerzug cemetery (Magyar Nemzeti Muzeum, Budapest); and from the Hallstatt Age settlement of Velemszentvid (Savaria Muzeum, Szombathely). In addition to the above, Professor V. I. Žalkin put at our disposal the measurements not published in full detail so far of a great number of Scythian horses from the south of Russia. Mrs. A. Paul-Bolomey made available to us the measurements of some horse bones originating from Histria, Rumania, the Greek colonial town on the Black Sea, while we ourselves measured at the Institute Zoologii A.N., U.S.S.R. (the Zoological Institute of the Academy of Sciences of the Soviet Union) in Leningrad the bone remains of sev-

eral horses originating from the Scythian kurgans of Central Asia. These were originally published by Vitt, who, however, did not publish their measurements. Since only the average and extreme values of the measurements of bone remains from Southern Russian and Central Asia have been published so far but not all their measurements, we publish them in the tables of the present work to enable other authors to make use of them in their further investigations.

BONE MATERIAL PUBLISHED HERE FOR THE FIRST TIME

1. Magdalenska Gora

The material comes from a cemetery of the Hallstatt Age, excavated by the Duchess of Mecklenburg, in 1914 (Hoernes, 1915).

a. *Tumulus IV, grave 43.* (Peabody Museum number: 34.25.40/7678.)
1. Fragment of os frontale.
2. Fragment of os occipitale.
3. 5 (2 left and 3 right) upper milk-premolars.
4. 2 (left and right) upper premolars.
5. 2 fragments of upper premolars.
6. 4 (2 left and 2 right) upper molars.
7. 2 fragments of mandible.
8. Milk I_3.
9. 4 (2 left and 2 right) lower milk-premolars.
10. 2 (left and right) lower P_1-s.
11. 4 (2 left and 2 right) lower molars.
12. Fragment of a molar.
13. Fragment of atlas.
14. 2 fragments of cervical vertebrae.
15. 6 fragments of thoracal vertebrae.
16. 4 fragments of vertebrae.
17. Fragment of a vertebra.
18. Fragment of a rib.
19. Articular end of the right scapula.
20. 2 fragments of scapulae.
21. 2 (left and right) proximal fragments of humeri.
22. 2 (left and right) distal halves of humeri.
23. Proximal fragment of the right radius.
24. 2 (left and right) distal ends of radii.
25. 2 (left and right) fragments of ulnae.
26. 2 (left and right) metacarpi.

27. Fragment of the left anterior os phalangis I.
28. Left anterior os phalangis II.
29. 4 (2 left and 2 right) hip-bones.
30. Right femur.
31. Distal part of the left femur.
32. Fragment of the proximal end of the left femur.
33. 2 (left and right) patellae.
34. Left tibia.
35. Right tibia.
36. 2 (left and right) astragali.
37. 2 (left and right) calcanei.
38. 10 carpal and tarsal bones.
39. 2 (left and right) metatarsi.
40. 2 (left and right) posterior ossa phalangis I.
41. 2 (left and right) posterior ossa phalangis II.

The molars and premolars, the end of scapula, the distal ends of humeri, the patellae, the astragali, the calcanei, the carpals and tarsals and the ends of metapodials and phalanges are damaged, the fragments of femora and the tibiae are restored from pieces and incomplete.

The skeleton is from a 3½- to 4½-year-old horse. The sex of the animal is undeterminable. The enamel pattern of the upper molars is simple, the extremity bones are slender.

From this grave came also 9 (7 left and 2 right) fragments of astragali, 2 (left and right) fragments of calcanei and a left os centrotarsale; they derive from 7-8 adult cattle (*Bos taurus* L.).

b. *Tumulus V, grave 5.* (P.M. number: 34.-25.40/7682.)

1. Right upper M_3.
2. Right lower M_2.

The roots of both the molars are damaged, their grinding surfaces are moderately waved.

The teeth come from an adult horse. The sex is undeterminable.

c. *Tumulus V, grave 29.* (P.M. number: 34.25.40/7679.)

Horse 1
1. Fragment of os occipitale and parietale.
2. 9 fragments of skull.
3. Fragment of left maxilla with the P_2-M_2.
4. Fragment of right maxilla with the M_1-M_3.
5. Right upper P_3.
6. Fragment of mandible with the left P_1-M_3.
7. 9 fragments of mandibles.
8. Lower right P_2.
9. Lower right P_3.
10. Lower right M_2.
11. Atlas.
12. 2 cervical vertebrae.
13. 2 fragments of cervical vertebrae.
14. Fragment of a thoracal vertebra.
15. Thoracal vertebra.
16. 2 thoracal vertebrae.
17. 6 thoracal vertebrae.
18. 2 lumbar vertebrae.

FIG. 1. Mandible of Horse I from grave 29, Tumulus V, Magdalenska gora.

19. 2 fragments of os sacrum.
20. 2 (left and right) distal parts of scapulae.
21. Fragment of right scapula.
22. 2 (left and right) humeri.
23. 2 (left and right) radii with fragments of ulnae.
24. Proximal part of left ulna.
25. Left metacarpal with the mc_2 and mc_4.
26. Right metacarpal with the mc_2 and mc_4.
27. 4 (2 left and 2 right) fragments of os coxae.
28. Left femur.
29. Right femur.
30. Left tibia.
31. Right tibia.
32. Right astragalus.
33. Right calcaneus.
34. Left metatarsal.
35. Right metatarsal.

The teeth are damaged with frequent lack of dentine and enamel; on their sides, mainly on the buccal surface, are tartar deposits. The oral part of the lower P_1-s is abraded nearly to the root (fig. 1). Several teeth are restored from fragments. Also the atlas and the cervical vertebrae are damaged, the thoracal vertebrae are ossified together, on their arcus, corpus and transverse processes are exostoses (figs. 2,3). The diaphysis and ends of the extremity bones are damaged, the right metacarpal and the left metatarsal are restored from fragments. On the dorsal surface of the left metatarsal, in the middle of the bone there is a rough exostosis.

The skeleton is that of an old stallion. The enamel pattern of the upper molars and premolars is simple, the protoconus is long. The ventral edge of the mandible is convex, with several exostoses on it.

Horse II
1. 6 (3 left and 3 right) upper incisors.
2. 2 (left and right) upper eye-teeth (dentes canini).
3. 6 (3 left and 3 right) upper premolars.
4. 6 (3 left and 3 right) upper molars.
5. Fragment of the right mandible with the P_1.
6. Fragment of the left mandible with the M_1-M_3.
7. Fragment of the right mandible with the M_2 and M_3.
8. 5 fragments of mandible.
9. 5 (3 left and 2 right) lower premolars.
10. Right lower M_1.
11. Atlas.
12. Axis.
13. 4 cervical vertebrae.
14. 2 fragments of cervical vertebrae.
15. 14 thoracal vertebrae.

16. 4 fragments of thoracal vertebrae.
17. 5 lumbar vertebrae.
18. 5 fragments of os sacrum.
19. 4 rib-fragments.
20. Distal part of left scapula.
21. 2 fragments of scapula.
22. Left humerus.
23. Right humerus.
24. Left radius with the fragment of ulna.
25. Proximal part of right radius with the fragment of ulna.
26. Distal fragment of right radius.
27. 2 (left and right) fragments of ulnae.
28. 2 (left and right) metacarpals.
29. Left anterior os phalangis I.
30. Left anterior os phalangis II.
31. Right anterior os phalangis III.
32. Fragment of left anterior os phalangis III.
33. 5 fragments of os coxae.
34. 2 (left and right) femora.
35. 2 (left and right) patellae.
36. 2 (left and right) tibiae.
37. 2 (left and right) metatarsals.
38. Fragment of a side-metapodial.
39. 2 (left and right) posterior ossa phalangis I.
40. Left posterior os phalangis II.
41. Left posterior os phalangis III.

One of the mandible-fragments is restored from fragments, the teeth are damaged, the oral part of P_1-s is considerably abraded. The ends of the extremity bones are generally damaged, the left metacarpal and the right femur are restored from fragments.

This is the skeleton of an adult, approximately 9-year-old stallion. The molars and premolars have a simple enamel pattern, their protoconus is long. The extremity bones are slender. The anterior hoof-bone has a flat sole; the posterior one is hollowed.

Horse III
1. Fragment of distal end of scapula.
2. Proximal end of left femur.
3. Distal part of left femur.
4. Left tibia.
5. Proximal end of right tibia.
6. Distal part of right tibia.
7. Diaphysis-fragment of right tibia.
8. Left astragalus.
9. 2 (left and right) calcanei.
10. Right metatarsal.

The astragalus, the calcanei and the ends of the long bones are damaged. The right calcaneus is restored from fragments.

Fig. 2. Vertebrae with pathological alterations of horse I from grave 29, Tumulus V, Magdalenska gora. Left side.

These are parts of the skeleton of an adult horse. The sex is undeterminable.

Horse IV
Distal part of right tibia. Its distal end is damaged. The bone comes from an adult horse. Its sex is undeterminable.

Also such horse bones from this grave came to light; about these one cannot decide to which of the four horses of the grave they belong. These are as follows:

1. 15 carpal and tarsal bones.
2. 3 fragments of side-metapodials.
3. Right anterior os phalangis I.
4. Right posterior os phalangis I.
5. Left posterior os phalangis I.
6. Left anterior os phalangis I.

The ends of the phalanges are damaged.

d. *Tumulus VII, grave 31.* (P.M. number: 34.25.40/7684).

Fragment of left astragalus. It is a bone of a young horse. The sex is undeterminable.

Also the left skull-fragment of an adult roe-deer *(Capreolus capreolus L.)* came to light from this grave.

e. *Tumulus VII, grave 38.* (P.M. number: 34.25.40/7685.)

Distal end of left tibia. It is damaged and restored from fragments.
It is a bone of a young horse. Its sex is undeterminable.

Also from this grave a left skull-fragment of an adult roe deer *(Capreolus capreolus L.)* came to light.

f. *Tumulus X, grave 14.* (P.M. number: 34.25.40/7680.)

Left lower M_3. Its crown and roots are damaged.

FIG. 3. Vertebrae with pathological alterations of Horse I from grave 29, Tumulus V, Magdalenska gora. Right side.

The tooth belongs to an adult horse. The sex is undeterminable.

g. *Tumulus X, grave 18.* (P.M. number: 34.25.40/7680).

Left upper premolar. Its root is damaged, on the labial surface there is a thick deposit of tartar.

It comes from an adult horse. The sex is undeterminable.

It is a small tooth, its enamel pattern is simple, the protoconus is very short.

h. *Tumulus X, grave 28.* (P.M. number: 34.25.40/7680.)

Right upper M_3. Its root is damaged.

It comes from an adult horse. The sex is undeterminable.

Also it is a small tooth with a simple enamel pattern of the grinding surface.

2. STIČNA, THE CEMETERY AT ŠENTVID

The bone material comes from a Hallstatt Age cemetery, which belongs to the well-known site of Stična. Excavated by the Duchess of Mecklenburg.

a. *Tumulus IV,*[1] *grave 16.*

1. Fragment of left upper P_3.
2. Fragment of left upper M_1.
3. Fragment of left upper M_2.
4. Right upper P_3.
5. Right upper M_1.
6. Right upper M_2.
7. Right upper M_3.
8. 3 fragments of upper molars.
9. Left lower P_2.
10. Left lower M_1.
11. Left lower M_2.
12. Left lower M_3.
13. Fragment of left lower P_3.
14. Right lower P_3.
15. Right lower M_1.

[1] Also called Tumulus Trondel.

16. Right lower M_2.
17. Right lower M_3.
18. Fragment of a lower premolar.
19. Rib-fragment.
20. Distal part of left scapula.
21. Fragment of right humerus.

The teeth are damaged.

There are parts of the skeleton of an adult horse. The sex is undeterminable.

The enamel pattern of the upper molars and premolars is simple, their protoconus is quite short.

b. *Tumulus IV, grave 47.* (P.M. number: 34.25.40/7687.)

1. 7 maxillar fragments.
2. 2 (left and right) upper P_2-s.
3. 2 (left and right) upper P_3-s.
4. 2 (left and right) upper M_1-s.
5. 2 (left and right) upper M_2-s.
6. 2 (left and right) upper M_3-s.
7. 4 fragments of a right tibia.

The roots of the teeth and the crowns of the right ones are damaged, on their labial surfaces there are thick deposits of tartar.

They are remains of an adult horse. The sex is undeterminable.

The teeth are small, their enamel pattern is simple.

3. BREZJE

From this cemetery of the Hallstatt Age we have horse bone material from two graves of a tumulus. Excavated by B. Pečnik (Kromer, 1959).

Tumulus VI, grave 1–2.

Horse I.
1. 2 skull-fragments.
2. 2 (left and right) fragments of mandible with the P_1-M_3.
3. Atlas.
4. Axis.
5. Distal part of left humerus.
6. 2 (left and right) radii.
7. Proximal part of left metacarpal.
8. Proximal part of left femur.
9. Distal part of right femur.

The teeth, the atlas, the axis and the ends of the long bones are damaged.

These remains are parts of the skeleton of an adult horse. The sex is undeterminable.

The skull has a broad forehead, the teeth are medium-sized, with simple enamel pattern and very long protoconus.

Horse II
1. Right upper P_3.
2. Right upper M_1.
3. Right upper M_2.
4. Right upper M_3.
5. Part of left mandible with the P_1-M_3.
6. Part of right mandible with the P_2-M_3.
7. Fragment of atlas.

The upper molars are damaged.

These are parts of an adult horse's skeleton. The sex is undeterminable.

The teeth are of medium size, their enamel pattern is simple, their protoconus is very long.

Horse III
Fragment of right radius.
It comes from a young horse of undeterminable sex.

4. TÁPIÓSZELE

It is a Scythian cemetery. Excavated by A. Bottyán, in 1937.

Grave 145. (Hungarian National Museum number: 61.1.1-3.Z.)

1. Skull.
2. Mandible with both P_1-P_3, M_2, M_3.
3. Fragment of mandible.

The skull and the mandible are damaged and restored from fragments. They are from a 3½- to 4-year-old stallion.

The skull is small, not very broad. Its front and profile-line are moderately convex, its brain-case is rather vaulted. The orbits are medium-sized, longitudinally oval. The lineae semicirculares are hardly projecting. The teeth are small, their enamel pattern is simple.

5. SZENTES-VEKERZUG

G. Csallány excavated a Scythian cemetery here in 1937 and 1941 and unearthed 11 graves.

The greater part of the cemetery was excavated by M. Párducz in 1950–54. Besides the human graves M. Párducz found a wagon with two horses and 10 horse graves with 12 skeletons. (Párducz, 1952; 1954; 1955; Bökönyi, 1952; 1954; 1955).

We publish a skeleton which was excavated by G. Csallány.

Grave 6 or 8. (H.N.M. number: 61.37.1-21.Z.)

1. 5 (3 left and 2 right) upper premolars.
2. Left upper molar.
3. Fragment of mandible.
4. 3 incisors.
5. 4 (2 left and 2 right) lower premolars.
6. Fragment of thoracal vertebra.
7. 2 rib-fragments.
8. Distal part of left scapula.
9. 2 (left and right) humeri.
10. 2 (left and right) radii with fragments of ulnae.
11. 2 (left and right) metacarpals.
12. 2 (left and right) anterior ossa phalangis I.
13. Left anterior os phalangis II.
14. Fragment of os coxae.
15. Right femur.
16. Fragment of caput femoris.
17. 2 (left and right) tibiae.
18. 2 (left and right) astragali.
19. Left calcaneus.
20. 2 (left and right) metatarsals.
21. Left posterior os phalangis I.

The short bones and the ends of the long bones are damaged.

They are parts of a 5- to 7-year-old horse. Its sex is undeterminable.

The teeth are small, with simple enamel pattern and with short protoconus. The extremity bones are slender.

6. Velemszentvid

It is a Hallstatt Age settlement, which extends over the La Tène period too. Excavated by K. Miske (Miske, 1896; 1907; 1908; Benda, 1928; Foltiny, 1958).

1. Left posterior os phalangis III. (Savaria Museum number: 8.)
2. Left upper premolar. (S.M. number: 30.)
3. Left upper M_3. (S.M. number: 31.)
4. Left radius with fragment of ulna. (S.M. number: 54.448.1.)
5. Right posterior os phalangis III. (S.M. number: 54.449.1.)
6. Left posterior os phalangis III. (S.M. number: 54.449.2.)
7. Incisor. (S.M. number: 54.481.1.)
8. 7 upper molars and premolars. (S.M. number: 54.482.1–7.)
9. 8 lower molars and premolars. (S.M. number: 54.483.1–8.)
10. Proximal part of right radius with fragment of ulna. (S.M. number: 54.484.1.)
11. Distal part of left radius. (S.M. number: 54.484.2.)
12. Right radius with fragment of ulna. (S.M. number: 54.484.3.)
13. Distal part of right tibia. (S.M. number: 54.485.1.)
14. Left astragalus. (S.M. number: 54.486.1.)
15. Fragment of os coxae. (S.M. number: 54.487.1.)
16. Right tibia. (S.M. number: 54.494.1.)
17. Left tibia. (S.M. number: 54.494.2.)

The crowns and roots of teeth, the short bones and the ends of long bones are damaged.

All bones come from adult horses. Their sex is undeterminable.

The premolars and molars are small or medium-sized, their enamel pattern is simple, the extremity bones are long and slender.

CHAPTER IV

DISCUSSION OF THE DATA OF MEASUREMENTS

WHEN elaborating the above-mentioned bone material, both that already published and that now published for the first time, it would be the most obvious way to start from the skull or from the results of the measurements carried out on them respectively. And yet, for two reasons we shall not pursue this way. The first reason is that, although the material at our disposal was immense, skulls, or parts of skulls suitable for comparison in it were rare. Thus, e.g., among the 13,019 horse remains found on the Iron Age excavation sites on the northern region of the Black Sea and elaborated by Zalkin (1960), there was not a single skull or large part of a skull, whereas an ample material is needed to carry out investigations of the skull. By the way, the Iron Age material of Jugoslavia and Hungary only contains one complete skull, and only parts of skulls and some teeth. The other reason, almost of equal importance with the former, is the circumstance that unfortunately so far there has not emerged a method of craniometry by which the differences of breeds and types—if they exist at all—could be demonstrated on the skulls of domestic horses. Therefore the skulls found in the material discussed here are only to be touched upon. We shall first and foremost only point to such characteristics by which they are reminiscent of horses' skulls originating from other European sites of a similar period.

Concerning the complete skull to be found in our material, which originates from the Scythian cemetery of Tápiószele, we can only say that it is very similar to the skulls of the Scythian horses of Szentes-Vekerzug. It is characterized by a broad front, a long cerebral and a short facial part, by a spacious and domed brain-case and by large orbits, rising above the plane of the front. With its frontal index of 43.8, the skull, according to the Gromova (1949) classification, belongs to the medium front group, thus to the same as the Scythian horses of Szentes-Vekerzug (Bök-

önyi, 1954), the two tarpans of Southern Russia as well as the greatest part of the Altaian Scythian horses of Vitt and Zalkin. The extant skull parts of the horses of Magdalenska gora and of Brezje also suggest broad fronts and well-developed cerebral skulls; however, on account of the smallness of the fragments with them we can neither refer to absolute measurements nor to attributes. The molars are generally small, with the exception of the Brezje horses, whose molars are of medium size. The dental enamel pattern is simple, the breadth of the enamel lines is even all along; the protoconus is long in the bulk of the cases. Some former authors considered the pattern of enamel lines as suited to discrimination between races, nay even species. Thus Rütimeyer (1863) based the separation of fossil species of horses on the differences of the molar enamel pattern, while Franck and Wilckens marked oriental horses off from occidental ones on grounds of the simpler or more complex enamel pattern. But Hilzheimer refuted these views as early as in 1912. He explained that the pattern of dental enamel is a function of the size of the tooth. The enamel pattern of smaller teeth is simpler while that of larger ones is more intricate. However, Lundholm joined issue with Hilzheimer's view, referring to the well-known fact that the enamel pattern of the Mongolian wild horse (= taki = *Equus przewalskii* Polj.) is simple, although its teeth are definitely large. It has become increasingly apparent that the enamel pattern is subject to strong individual variability (Nobis, 1962). On grounds of the Hungarian material from the time of the post-Roman folk migration we have gained the same experience: in the same cemetery we have found horses of largely the same age, the same structure of skull and the same dimensions of the extremities whose enamel patterns were of the greatest variety of different types. We consider in more or less the same way the question of a long or short protoconus, particularly on the premolars, which

18

parallel with the animal's aging gets proportionally shorter and in the case of old animals is quite similar to that of asses. This fact also shows that from the mere shortness or length of the protoconus on the premolars it cannot be decided whether they belonged to horses or asses. There is another noteworthy characteristic to be found on teeth in our material: both on the upper and the lower molars there is a thick layer of cement, which could be observed earlier on the Szentes-Vekerzug horses too (Bökönyi, 1954; 1955). This is a characteristic attributed to steppe horses though not investigated in detail so far.

Having surveyed in short the skulls let us now discuss the measurements of the bones of extremities, which are meant to constitute the core of our present investigations. When investigating the bones of extremities we shall not only discuss the material published now for the first time but deal in similar detail with measurements drawn from literature already published, measurements made available to us by the kindness of foreign colleagues, and taken or completed by ourselves. It is the aim of these investigations to determine in our material the possible groups of horses of the Iron Age and, if such groups can be demonstrated, to determine their characteristics, the differences or similarities between them, their possible effect upon each other, their spread both in space and in time, etc.

Among the extremity bones, we have used for the purposes of these examinations the metapodia, these being the strongest and most resistant bones of the skeleton. For these very qualities they are most frequent in nearly every archaeological site and are relatively intact even in settlements. There is practically no flesh on them, and their marrow content is very small, for, because of their thick walls, their cavum medullare is little. That is why they had not been broken open. However, we have also used other extremity bones to be able to include in our comparisons horses from earlier excavations when, due to the shortcomings of collecting, the material did not contain any metapodia, e.g., Brezje horses. For this purpose we have chosen another extremity bone, the radius, which is not very liable to damage either.

On grounds of the diagrams of the metapodia it can be stated that the Iron Age horses of Central and Eastern Europe were by no means uniform but formed two groups, which can be clearly divided from one another. The Scythian and Greek horses of Southern Russia, the Thracian horses of Bulgaria, the horses from the sixth century B.C. of Histria in Rumania, the Scythian horses of Hungary as well as the horses of the Hallstatt Age of Magdalenska gora and of Brezje belong to the first group, whereas the horses of the Hallstatt Age of Austria and Germany and of the La Tène Age of Germany and Switzerland constitute the second. The remains of horses from Stična (Šentvid) were too fragmentary to be placed in either group. The Scythian horses of South Russia and also the horses of the Scythian kurgans of the Altaian area are well related to the first group. As is evident from the above, the two groups are well separated geographically, too, since the first extends over the eastern part of Europe. For this reason we shall indicate it, for simplicity's sake, as "eastern group" without wishing to identify it with the oriental type of horses of Franck, whereas the second extends over the western part of Central Europe, and for this reason we shall call it in the following "the western group," but do not identify it with Franck's occidental type of horses.

First of all there is a difference in size between the horses of the two groups. In the eastern group the greatest length of the metacarpals is between 198–245, the average being 220.62, whereas 174.5 to 236.5 with an average of 197.75 mm. applies to the western group. Figure 4 and the following table show the division of the measurements.

Length	171-175	176-180	181-185	186-190	191-195	196-200	201-205	206-210	211-215	216-220	221-225	226-230	231-235	236-240	241-245	N
Eastern group	0	0	0	0	0	2	5	11	24	38	35	34	10	4	5	168
Western group	1	4	10	16	24	22	35	12	7	5	0	1	0	1	0	138
Total number of bones	1	4	10	16	24	24	40	23	31	43	35	35	10	5	5	306

METACARPUS

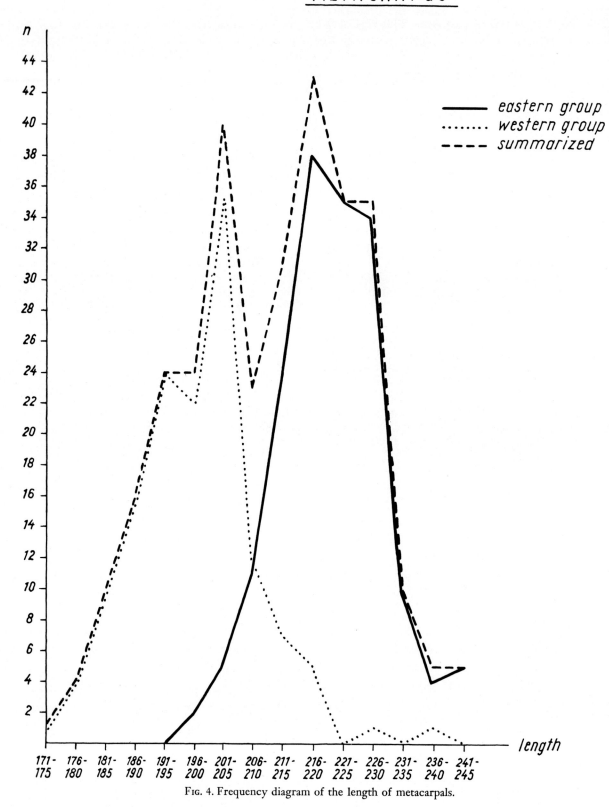

Fig. 4. Frequency diagram of the length of metacarpals.

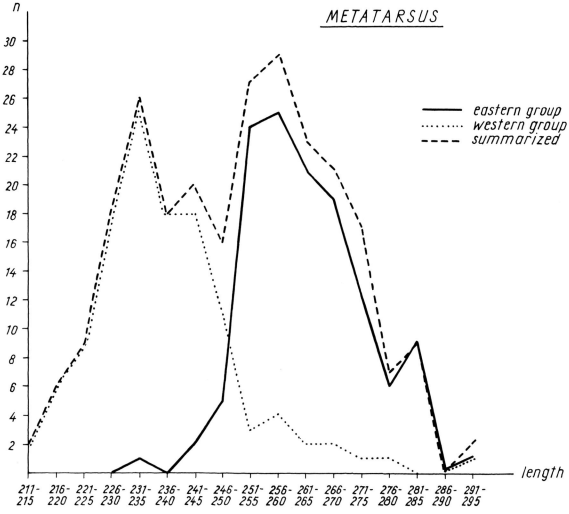

FIG. 5. Frequency diagram of the length of metatarsals.

With the eastern group the greatest length of the metatarsals is 234–294 with an average of 262.85, and 214–291 with an average of 237.38 mm. applies to the western group. Figure 5 and the following table show the division of the measurements.

Length	211-215	216-220	221-225	226-230	231-235	236-240	241-245	246-250	251-255	256-260	261-265	266-270	271-275	276-280	281-285	286-290	291-295	N
Eastern group	0	0	0	0	1	0	2	5	24	25	21	19	16	6	9	0	1	129
Western group	2	6	9	18	25	18	18	11	3	4	2	2	1	1	0	0	1	121
Total number of bones	2	6	9	18	26	18	20	16	27	29	23	21	17	7	9	0	2	250

The two diagrams and the tables evince that the stock consists of two groups, out of which the eastern is that of larger-bodied and the western that of smaller-bodied animals. For reasons to be detailed further on, there is some overlapping of the two groups, which, however, is minimal, because in the case of the metacarpals the lowest value of the eastern group is higher than the average of the western group, and in the case of the metatarsals it is only lower by three mm. Moreover only very few extreme values of one group overlap into the variation width of the other. The foregoing are supported by the measurements published about the horses of the territories where animals of the western group were prevalent. We could not include these measurements in our statistics since the authors only indicated the extreme measurements and not those of the several bones. Schwerz's data about the La Tène horses belong here: the longest metacarpals are 206 and the longest metatarsals 235 mm. With them the largest metacarpal measurement hardly exceeds the average of the western group, while the metatarsal measurements do not even come up to them.

According to the aforesaid, the above groups constitute well definable, independent units. But a more detailed evaluation of the diagram peaks is not so easy. In the case of these peaks we may think of differences in sex; however, the proportion of stallions and mares represented by the metacarpals and metatarsals respectively appears in a reverse way. With the western group the stallions are more frequently represented by metacarpals and the mares by metatarsals, whereas with the eastern group mares are more frequently represented by metacarpals and stallions by metatarsals.

The independent character of the two groups of horses determined on the basis of the length of the metapodia can be supported by mathematical-statistical methods too. This can be done by means of two tests, the so-called t and f tests. The result of the t test

$$t = \frac{M_1 - M_2}{\sqrt{\dfrac{s_1^2}{N_1} + \dfrac{s_2^2}{N_2}}}$$

is 18.639 with the metacarpals and 11.371 with the metatarsals, which means that the probability of the two groups belonging together is much less than 0.1% (P<< 0.1). The difference of values referring to the metacarpals and to the metatarsals at the same time also means that on grounds of the metatarsals the separate and independent character of the two groups is to a minimal extent more explicit, i.e., Sickenberg's view has been proved according to which metatarsals are always more characteristic of groups of horses since they are far less subject to individual variability.

The result of the f test, $f = \dfrac{s_1^2}{s_2^2}$ is 1.388 with the metarcarpals and 1.613 with the metatarsals. Similarly to the t test these values too evince the actual existence of the two independent groups.

As mentioned above, in some sites there were no metapodia to be found but there were radii, though they were relatively less frequent. For this reason we have used the measurements of the latter bone in our investigations too. With the eastern group the highest length of the radius is 307–375, the average being 330.86, and with the western group 280–335, the average being 304.53 mm. Figure 6 and the following table show the division of values:

Length	281-290	291-300	301-310	311-320	321-330	331-340	341-350	351-360	361-370	371-380	N
Eastern group	0	0	1	6	9	8	2	0	2	1	29
Western group	6	15	11	5	2	2	0	2	0	0	43
Total number of bones	6	15	12	11	11	10	2	2	2	1	72

The above also demonstrate the independent character of the two groups, although on one hand the results are not so convincing because of the smaller number of pieces and, on the other, the difference is somewhat slighter, which is shown also by the result 6.75 of the

RADIUS

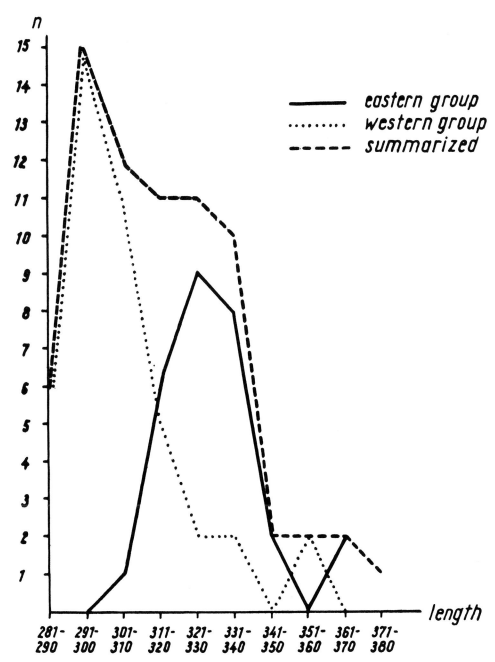

FIG. 6. Frequency diagram of the length of radii.

SLENDERNESS - INDEX OF METACARPALS

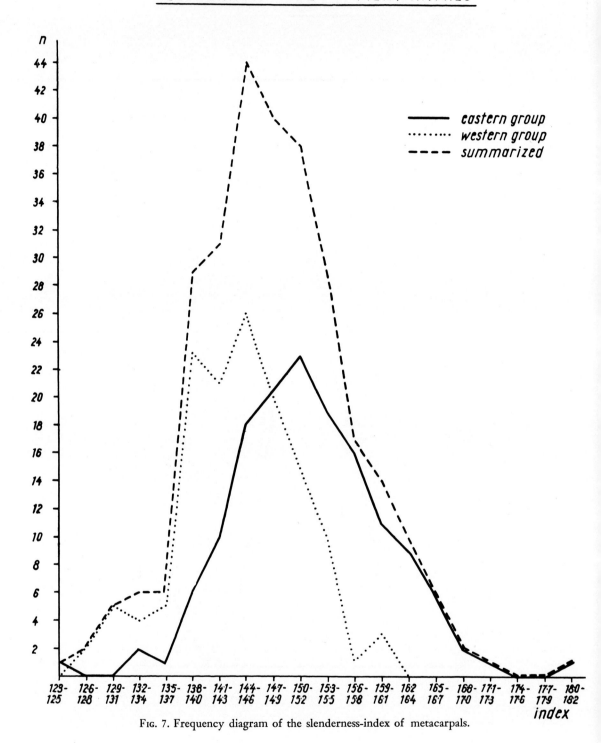

FIG. 7. Frequency diagram of the slenderness-index of metacarpals.

t test; nevertheless even here the possibility of a correspondence is below 0.1%.

Now the question arises whether the two groups of horses determined on grounds of length measurements differ also on the basis of the slenderness relations of the long bones and first of all of the metapodia, and, if they do, of what the difference consists. To decide this question we examined the slenderness indices of the metapodia (smallest breadth of the diaphysis x 100/highest length of the bone). The picture gained with the metacarpals is the following (see fig. 7):

Index	12.3-12.5	12.6-12.8	12.9-13.1	13.2-13.4	13.5-13.7	13.8-14.0	14.1-14.3	14.4-14.6	14.7-14.9	15.0-15.2	15.3-15.5	15.6-15.8	15.9-16.1	16.2-16.4	16.5-16.7	16.8-17.0	17.1-17.3	17.4-17.6	17.7-17.9	18.0-18.2	N
Eastern group	1	0	0	2	1	6	10	18	20	23	19	16	11	9	6	2	1	0	0	1	146
Western group	0	2	5	4	5	23	21	26	20	15	10	1	3	1	0	0	0	0	0	0	136
Total no. of bones	1	2	5	6	6	29	31	44	40	38	29	17	14	10	6	2	1	0	0	1	282

Thus with the metacarpals of the eastern group the smallest values of the slenderness index is 12.5 and the biggest 18.1, the average being 15.190, whereas with that of the western group the corresponding values are 12.7, 16.2 and 14.513 respectively.

On the other hand the metatarsals give the following picture (see fig. 8):

Index	10.0-10.2	10.3-10.5	10.6-10.8	10.9-11.1	11.2-11.4	11.5-11.7	11.8-12.0	12.1-12.3	12.4-12.6	12.7-12.9	13.0-13.2	13.3-13.5	13.6-13.8	13.9-14.1	N
Eastern group	0	2	5	10	17	21	24	16	9	3	3	1	4	3	118
Western group	3	8	13	23	33	17	13	6	1	0	0	0	0	0	117
Total number of bones	3	10	18	33	50	38	37	22	10	3	3	1	4	3	235

Here the lowest value of the eastern group is 10.3, the highest value 14.0, the average being 11.93, while the values of the western group are the following: 10.0, 12.5 and 11.35 respectively.

When comparing the slenderness indices of the metapodia it can be stated that with respect to slenderness there cannot be such essential differences found as with respect to relationships of length, which means that both groups belong to the same growth type. The slight divergence that exists between the two groups in this field is just the opposite of what could have been expected. Formerly the widespread opinion prevailed in the literature of horse-breeding that the metapodia of oriental horses are slender whereas those of occidental ones are stocky. This opinion, of course, is rooted in the slenderness relations of today's horses, its basis being the Arab thoroughbred on one hand and the cold-blooded horse on the other. Well, here it is just the other way round: the metapodia of the eastern group are stockier and those of the western group more slender, although it must be emphasized again that the difference is a minimal one and on this basis the two groups cannot be divided. Nor have we found Gromova's (1949) assumption to be justified, according to which the lengthening of extremity bones goes parallel with their becoming slenderer, whereas their shortening is accompanied by their getting stockier within the *Equus* genus. On grounds of our material we have rather come to a conclusion similar to that of Nobis (1962), according to which the longer extremity bones are thicker and the shorter ones thinner.

The division of the metapodia of the two groups according to the Chersky classification is very interesting. On grounds of the slenderness index of the metacarpals Chersky divided horses into three groups. According to this

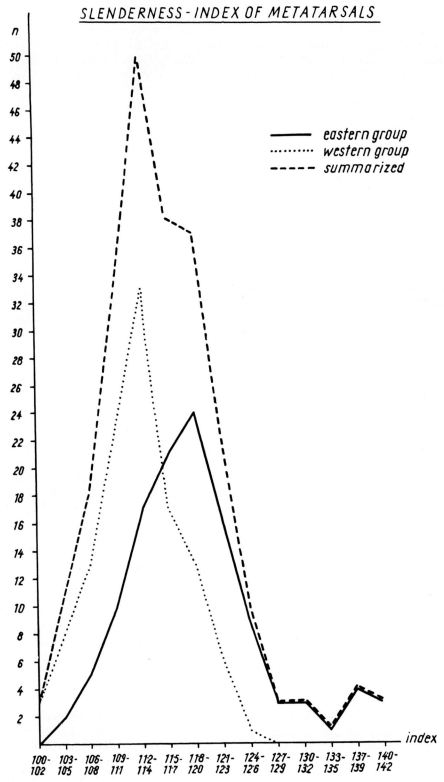

FIG. 8. Frequency of the slenderness-index of metatarsals.

grouping horses whose slenderness index is under 15.0 belong to the slender-legged group, those with an index between 15.1–17.0 to the medium-legged group and those with an index above 17.0 to the thick-legged group. According to Chersky's grouping the distribution of the horses of our two groups is the following:

		slender-legged	medium-legged	thick-legged
eastern group		58	86	2
	%	39.73	58.90	1.37
western group		106	30	0
	%	77.94	22.06	0

Essentially this distribution evinces the same as the two diagrams and tables above: the metacarpals of the western group are slenderer and on grounds of the slenderness index over three-quarters of the horses of this group belong to the slender-legged group, whilst not a single individual belongs to the thick-legged group; the metapodia of the eastern horses are relatively stockier, so their majority belongs to the medium-legged group and two horses to the thick-legged group.

In order to investigate the slenderness variation broken down to the metapodia we have prepared the following four diagrams (figs. 9–12). In them each metapodium that can be measured in its full length is indicated; the length measurements have been brought into comparison with the smallest breadth or the proximal end breadth respectively. Although we know that with the proximal breadth measurements used for comparisons the individual variability is greater than with the smallest breadth of the diaphysis, we brought into comparison the last above-mentioned measurement for the following reason and purpose:

1. Many authors do not use the measurement "smallest breadth of diaphysis" which we are using here but apply the measurement "breadth of diaphysis in the middle of the bone" instead. Other authors, particularly the older ones, do not take any measurements of the diaphysis at all; however, in order to be able to include in our investigations these authors' material too

and to make use of it in our comparisons we have compared here the length with the proximal end breadth. Besides, in the case of the measurements published by the former group of the above-mentioned authors we avoid erroneous comparisons which would originate from the fact that the breadth measurement taken in the middle of the diaphysis is somewhat larger than the smallest breadth of the diaphysis.

2. In this way we wish to enable such researchers to use our diagrams and to compare the bone measurements in a manner different from ours.

Regarding the separation of the two groups on the diagrams on grounds of the length measurements, the situation is absolutely clear, particularly on the diagram of the metatarsals, whilst the separation on the diagram of metacarpals is somewhat more difficult. The centers of interest for the two groups are indicated well by the spots where the values get denser. Out of the eastern group the Altaian and South Russian horses attract attention by the highest length measurements; they are followed by the Histrian horses and by the Thracian ones of Bulgaria; then come the Scythian horses of Hungary and the horses of Magdalenska gora. One of the latter is on the border of the western group, although right beside it, regarding the structure of the skull, there stands a typically eastern horse of Szentes-Vekerzug and an Altaian Scythian horse, whereas the metatarsal length of another Szentes-Vekerzug horse and a Scythian horse of the South of Russia is even smaller. In the western group the horses of Manching constitute a rather close block. This has been pointed out by Liepe and Frank, who elaborated them. Only a few individuals stand out from that block, one of which is the individual of the largest withers height among the horses discussed here. In the Manching group there are some definitely dwarfish individuals too—the smallest horses dealt with in our material. By their size these bones could belong to asses. This points to the fact that with certain metapodia it cannot be decided by mere measurements whether they originate from horses or from asses. In general the Swiss horses of the Iron Age belong to the Manching horses, and so do the La Tène horses of Schwertz, which do not figure in the diagrams.

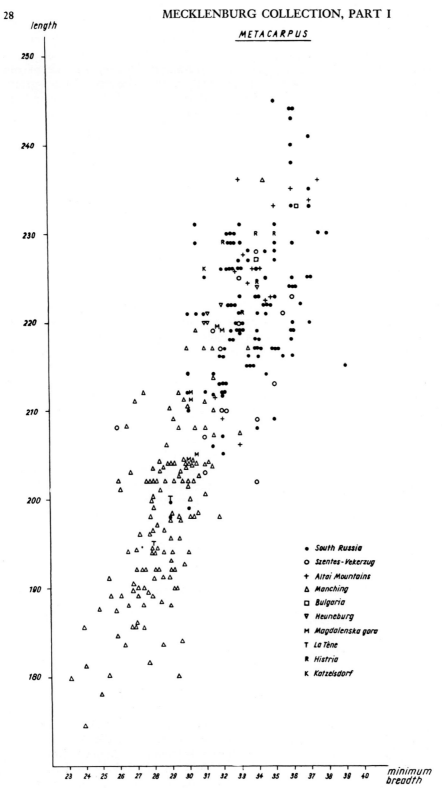

FIG. 9. Distribution of the relation between the length and minimum breadth of metacarpals.

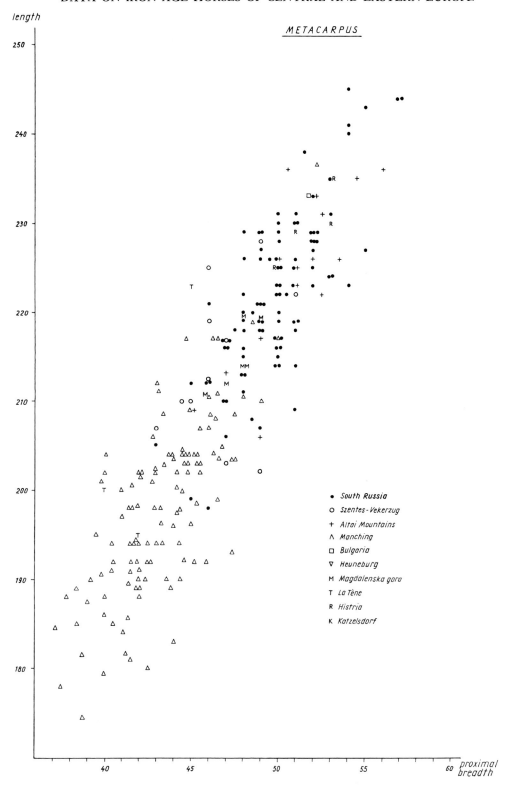

FIG. 10. Distribution of the relation between the length and proximal breadth of metacarpals.

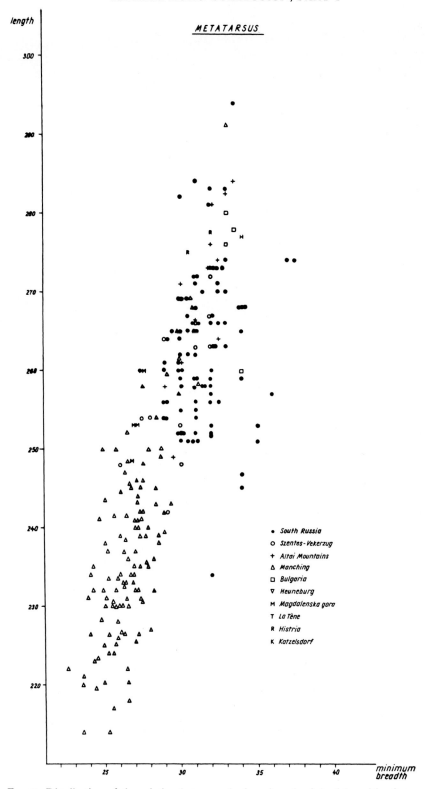

FIG. 11. Distribution of the relation between the length and minimal breadth of metatarsals.

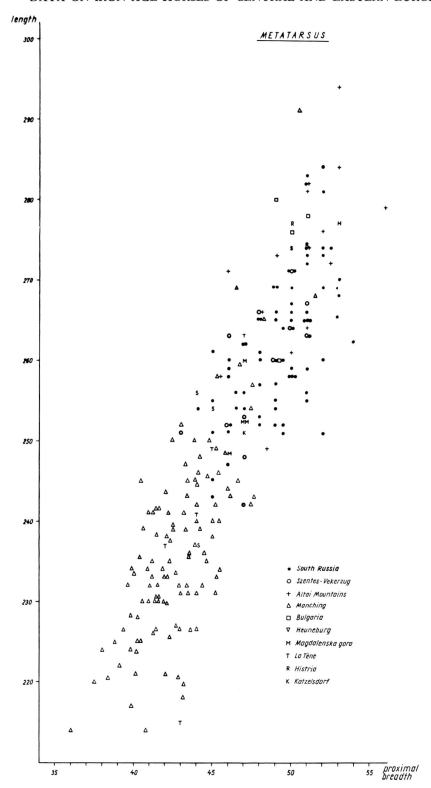

FIG. 12. Distribution of the relation between the length and proximal breadth of metatarsals.

The metapodia of one individual only fall into the lower part of the variation breadth of the eastern group. On the other hand, the Austrian horses of the Iron Age and the Heuneburg horses of the Hallstatt Age fall among the larger members of the western group or into the middle of the variation breadth of this group respectively. Nevertheless, owing to the small amount of material, this does not justify a generalization.

With respect to slenderness the first striking phenomenon is the fact that the western group is less variable than the eastern one, although it is not impossible that this homogeneity is due to the fact that the Manching horses make up the bulk of this group, i.e., the population consisting of a great number of individuals, evidently related to one another from a single archaeological site. The Scythian horses of Southern Russian can be considered as the most variable representatives of the eastern group. Among them, side by side with definitely slender individuals, there are some definitely thick-legged ones, particularly among the metatarsals. These, as it were, form a separate subgroup. The horses of the Altaian kurgans are somewhat more uniform from this point of view and, on the average, a tiny bit more slender than those of Southern Russia. The Thracian and Histrian horses, too, are uniform; the former are somewhat slenderer than the average of the eastern horses, the latter, along with the horses of Magdalenska gora, are very slender. The Scythian horses of Szentes-Vekerzug are rather variable; the horse with the slenderest metacarpal in the whole material elaborated here is among them, but there are also some individuals among them with stocky legs. Out of the western group the Manching horses are the most variable ones, which is obviously due to their great numbers. It was among them that the slenderest and also the thickest metapodium of the whole group were found. The Swiss horses of the Iron Age are in the middle of the variation; the Heuneburg horses are in one section, among the slender ones.

It is somewhat more difficult to separate the two groups on grounds of the relationship between length and proximal end breadth, particularly with the metacarpals. With respect to variability in the case of metacarpals the western and eastern groups are largely correspondent. Here too we can find some metacarpals from Scythian horses of southern Russia, although not so strikingly stocky. Besides, the picture tallies with that gained in comparing the length diaphysis—smallest breadth, the only strange feature being that one of the Swiss metacarpals shows, side by side with a medium diaphysis breadth, an outstandingly small proximal breadth, whereas with two metacarpals of Histria we have found, side by side with a thin diaphysis, a proximal end of medium thickness. As far as the metatarsals are concerned the variability of the eastern group is somewhat higher than that of the western one. Beside some strikingly stocky metatarsals of Scythian horses from Southern Russia, we can find similarly stocky pieces in the Manching population and the metatarsal of a Swiss horse of the Iron Age too shows great proximal breadth.

A similar picture is given by the radii, although with many fewer measurements. Their diagrams (figs. 13, 14), too, indicate the difference between the two groups. Here, too, the Scythian horses of Southern Russian show the largest measurements. We have no measurements of Altaian horses for this bone, but on grounds of the average values indicated by Vitt it can be stated that the horses of Pazyryk, on the basis of the measurements of this bone too, belong to the upper half of the variation breadth of the eastern group. So does one of the Brezje horses. One of the radii found at Velemszentvid is ranged in the upper half of the variation breadth of the eastern group and the other in its lowermost part beside the radius of one of the horses of Magdalenska gora. The other radius of Magdalenska gora which can be measured is on the border of the two groups along with a horse of Szentes-Vekerzug and a Scythian horse of Southern Russia; however, the radius of another Scythian horse of Southern Russia is even smaller—thus the situation is rather like the one regarding the metacarpal of the same horse. The smallest radii measurements are displayed by the Manching horses. The slenderness relations are rather variable; the thickness of the radii of a considerable part of the Scythian horses of Southern Russia is striking. On the other hand, three of their longest radii are very thin and

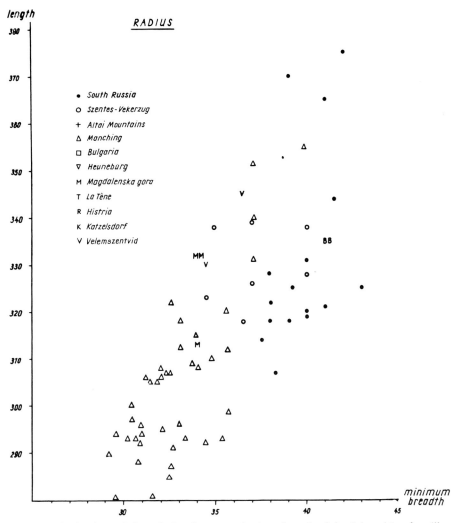

FIG. 13. Distribution of the relation between the length and minimal breadth of radii.

extraordinarily little in proximal breadth.

Two more striking phenomena can be observed on the above diagrams as well as on those indicating the slenderness relationship of the metapodia. One of them is that on grounds of the slenderness index we are unable to separate such units as could be considered groups of individuals of the same sex. According to a generally adopted opinion the extremity bones of individual horses of different sexes can be well divided on the basis that the bones of stallions are stockier than those of mares, whereas those of gelded animals excel by their length since with them the border of

epiphysis—diaphysis gets ossified rather late, thus the lengthwise growth of the bones with them lasts longer than with stallions and mares (Tschirwinsky). This question did not seem to be quite clarified to us even earlier (1954), when, with the Scythian horses of Szentes-Vekerzug the picture of the sex of the horses based on the slenderness indices of the extremity bones did not correspond with the one we had drawn up on grounds of the presence or absence of eyeteeth (dentes canini) or of the formation of the os coxae. At that time we did not deal with the question in detail. Later, however, Zalkin (1961) in the course of his

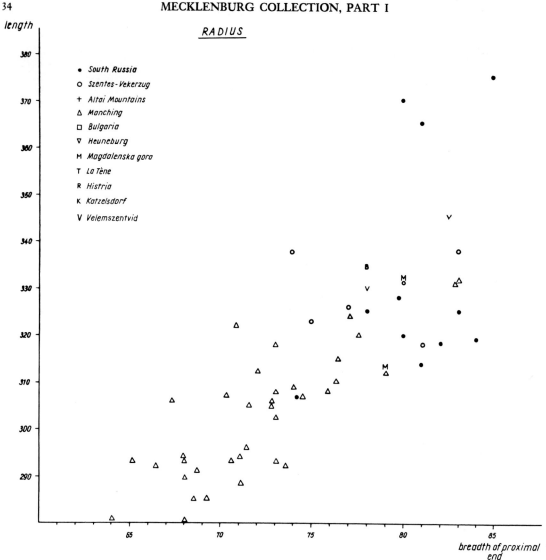

Fɪɢ. 14. Distribution of the relation between the length and proximal breadth of radii.

examinations of the metapodia of sheep, stated that the metapodials of rams and wethers cannot be distinguished even within the same breed, and even in the case of a rich material the bones of animals of different sexes cannot be separated on grounds of the slenderness index. Essentially the case is similar with cattle too (Zalkin, 1960; Bökönyi and Kubasiewicz, 1961), where the index limits of Nobis (1954) seem difficult to maintain. If the material in question originated only from cemeteries, the above phenomenon could be explained since it was mostly stallions and geldings that were found in graves; however, the bulk of the material originates from settlements which means that both sexes ought to be represented in it. Everything points to the fact that in the case of a large material of horses—similarly to that of sheep or cattle—the limits of sexes set up on grounds of slenderness comparisons are arbitrary ones and thus they overlap. This lessens the value of such experiments as are aimed at separating sexes on grounds of indices in case of a small material, the consequence being that no general limits valid for all populations can be set up. To determine sexes on grounds of the slenderness index in case of incomplete skeletons or separate bones continues to be questionable, and we shall have to rely on the well-proven distinguishing marks of the os coxae and on the presence or absence of eyeteeth, although the value of the latter has been markedly reduced by Habermehl's examinations according to which with 22 per cent of the mares of small-bodied breeds eyeteeth were present.

The other striking phenomenon to be observed on the above diagrams is the fact that within the two great groups no subgroups referring to smaller regional units can be demonstrated. It often happens that horses from neighboring territories show similar measurements as could be observed in the case of one of the Szentes-Vekerzug and of the Magdalenska gora horses, or in the case of the Bulgarian and Histrian horses. However, in the first case, close by them could be found the measurements of the Scythian horses of Southern Russia and in the second those of the Altaian horses.

Since the withers height of horses originating from subfossil finds can only be established on grounds of the length measurements of the bones, by multiplying them with certain index figures elaborated by Kiesewalter, differences of withers height between the two groups of horses discussed here should be similar to those we found on grounds of the length of the metapodia. It should be pointed out here that Vitt too elaborated a method for determining the withers height, which with quite minimal differences shows the same results as the Kiesewalter method. Müller (1955) elaborated another method applicable to skeletons lying *in situ*. This, however, cannot be used in the present case. For determining withers heights we are using here the Kiesewalter method exclusively, because this is the one used by the majority of authors, and by applying the same we wish to ensure the possibility of comparisons. In general one of the significant sources of mistakes in the methods for determining the withers height is the circumstance that the individual variability of the proportions of the length of different long bones is very high within the same breed and

even within the same population. We pointed this out when examining the horses of the Szentes-Vekerzug cemetery. The values of withers height calculated on grounds of the length of the different long bones of the horses found there strongly varied, and these values and those measured on the skeletons found *in situ* showed significant divergences (Bökönyi, 1954). Recently Nobis (1962) has stated that the real value of withers height can be reliably calculated only on grounds of the averages obtained from the length of all of the long bones. Setting out from Nobis's statement above, Villwock considers the calculation of withers height on grounds of isolated long bones as absolutely useless. Although we accept Nobis's statement, we by no means agree with Villwock's opinion for, if we did agree with it, we would have no possibility of stating the approximate withers height of the horses of the population of a settlement because on such sites no complete skeletons can be found but only separate bones. However, archaeological research is increasingly directed toward the excavation of settlements, for the living conditions of human beings of past ages can be best reconstructed from the materials of settlements and from the phenomena observed there and not on grounds of cemeteries which chiefly reflect the burial rituals. Thus, if we accepted Villwock's opinion we could not evaluate from the point of view of withers height the largest and most considerably increasing material, a material which represents the horse stock of a certain period without any selection as against the material of cemeteries in which we find individuals selected from the point of view of rituals, etc.; i.e., an arbitrarily selected part of the original population. In our opinion we cannot forego determining the withers height in case of single long bones, which do not belong to complete skeletons only because the method at our disposal is not quite perfect. Besides trying to bring to perfection the Kiesewalter method in some way or another, we must attempt to elaborate another method, approaching the question from another side and establishing the method on a different basis and, last but not least, we must use the data obtained by means of the existing method so as to be able to reconstruct biologically the material under investigation, approaching it from as many sides as possible. The only qualification to be applied is that the values of withers height obtained on grounds of solitary bones should be considered as having an informative character. From this point the application of the Vitt method might be better, since it is more flexible than the Kiesewalter one and does not supply indices but limit-values according to the groups of length measurements. Nevertheless, in case of large materials we may well use the Kiesewalter method even for materials from settlements, for in such cases the divergences get equalized,

and the withers height measurements obtained give as realistic a picture of the population as those calculated on grounds of all the long bones of a few skeletons. Setting out from the above reasoning we have calculated the values of withers height ourselves although the bulk of our material originated from settlements, i.e, we faced solitary bones and used the Kiesewalter method for our calculations.

The following two tables on grounds of metacarpals and metatarsals as well as figures 15 and 16 show the distribution of withers height values:

METACARPALS

Withers height	108-110	111-113	114-116	117-119	120-122	123-125	126-128	129-131	132-134	135-137	138-140	141-143	144-146	147-149	150-152	N
Eastern group	0	0	0	0	1	4	9	18	24	26	24	21	4	8	1	140
Western group	1	1	9	12	26	25	27	19	13	5	5	4	1	0	1	149
Total number of bones	1	1	9	12	27	29	36	37	37	31	29	25	5	8	2	289

METATARSALS

Withers height	111-113	114-116	117-119	120-122	123-125	126-128	129-131	132-134	135-137	138-140	141-143	144-146	147-149	150-152	153-155	N
Eastern group	0	0	0	1	0	2	10	31	24	17	11	8	9	1	0	114
Western group	3	6	13	19	26	22	15	11	4	2	3	1	0	0	1	126
Total number of bones	3	6	13	20	26	24	25	42	28	19	14	9	9	1	1	240

According to the foregoing, the withers height determined on grounds of the metacarpals is 121.1–149.4 cm. (the average being 136.15) with the eastern group, and 109.9–149.4 cm. (the average being 126.07) with the western group. The withers height determined on grounds of the metatarsals is 120.4–151.9 cm. (the average being 137.12) with the eastern group and 112.5–153.5 cm. (the average being 126.69) with the western group. Schwerz's material of La Tène not indicated here is to be added to the above. In that material the withers height based on the longest metacarpals is 129.5 cm. and on the metacarpals 120.4–123.2 cm. These values fall into the middle of the western group, or into the lower part of its size variations respectively. In the case of withers heights calculated on grounds of the metacarpals the t test referring to the separateness of the two groups is 18.362 and in case of withers heights calculated on grounds

of the metatarsals is 16.327; whereas the f test results in 1.380 and 1.487 respectively. Both tests prove the separate existence of the two groups.

Of course, the difference between the two groups is indicated by the different withers heights too, which amounted to about 10 cm. The fact that the difference of average withers height calculated on grounds of the length of the metacarpals and of the metatarsals respectively is only 0.62 with the western group and 0.97 cm. with the eastern group demonstrated that the calculation of withers height is justified even in case of solitary bones, provided they are found in a big material. Again, the fact that for both groups it was on grounds of the metatarsal length that the bigger withers height values were obtained, points to the direction in which the Kiesewalter indices are to be corrected.

However, the above tables and diagrams al-

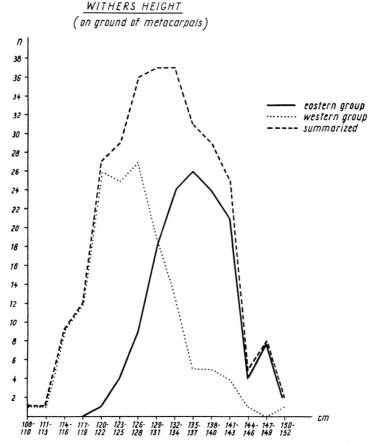

FIG. 15. Distribution of the withers height on ground of the length of metacarpals.

so indicate that the Kiesewalter method needs reshaping from another aspect too. The basis of this method is the relationship between the length measurements of the bones and the withers height, thus the frequency diagrams of bone measurements and the frequency diagrams of withers height should completely tally; similarly identical results ought to be obtained as a result of statistical examinations. This, however, is not the case. We have obtained on our length measurement diagrams (figs. 4, 5) definitely two-peaked curves, but the curves of the separate groups too have been definitely single ones, whereas in the withers height diagrams with the values calculated on grounds of metacarpals (fig. 15) the common curve is one-peaked, although rather drawn out sideways. Its "peak" is provided by three frequency values essentially identical, and the curves of the two groups strongly overlap each other. Although with the withers height values calculated on grounds of the metatarsals (fig. 16) the common curve is two-peaked, these peaks are not so markedly separated as in the diagram of the metatarsal length measurements (fig. 5); moreover the curves of the two groups overlap each other to some extent though not so much as in case of the metacarpals (fig. 15). The parallel to be observed in the diagrams of length measurements and withers heights shows that it is always with the metatarsals that the groups become more markedly differentiated. If, on the other hand, we investigate the reasons for the overlapping, i.e., why it is somewhat more difficult to separate the two groups on grounds of withers heights, we get the following result: the cause is to be found in the Kiesewalter method which does

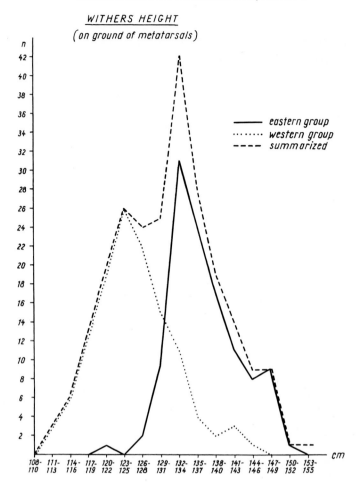

FIG. 16. Distribution of the withers height on ground of the length of metatarsals.

not take the greatest length of the bone as a basis upon which the withers height can be calculated but its lateral length. When elaborating the Szentes-Vekerzug horses, we erroneously multiplied the greatest length measurement, instead of the lateral length, by Kiesewalter's indices and thus obtained there withers height values higher than the real ones. As testified by tables of measurements the process pursued when taking lateral length measurements is not exactly identical with different authors: Zalkin and ourselves, e.g., obtained relatively lower values than Liepe and Frank, and since nine tenths of the measurements utilized in our study originate from these four authors, the differences in measuring techniques left their marks upon the withers height values obtained. This is easily understandable if we consider that, e. g., a divergence of 2 mm. resulted in a difference of about 13 mm. in the case of the metacarpals and of 10.5 mm. in the case of metatarsals when calculating the withers height. This again is a very good example of how important it is that when elaborating a large material, measurements should be taken by the same hands, as already suggested above. In order to abolish the aforementioned error, which, although insignificant, can give rise to misunderstandings, it would be worthwhile to redesign the Kiesewalter indices to the greatest length of the bones, a measurement which can be taken in one way only and which is generally adopted and used anyway.

Chapter V

DISCUSSION OF RESULTS

ON GROUNDS of the measurement relations discussed in the foregoing we can now state absolutely positively that the Iron Age horses of Central and Eastern Europe were not uniform but comprised two separate groups, which can be well separated from each other. We have tried to set up the two groups on a geographical basis separating the finds of the territories eastwards and westwards respectively from the approximate line of Vienna-Venice. The word groups we have used intentionally instead of the denominations "type" or "breed," since the former would refer to genetical differences and the latter to the assumption of planned stock-breeding, whereas neither appears to be proved. This division on a geographical basis has been proved on grounds of the measurement data and, to a certain extent, craniologically too. The members of the eastern group are the Iron Age horses of the eastern part of Central Europe, of Eastern and Southeastern Europe, while those of the western group are horses of the Iron Age originating from the western part of Central Europe. According to this, the former group comprises the Scythian and Hallstatt Age horses of Hungary (we have no useful horse finds from Hungary from the La Tène period), the horses of Magdalenska gora and Šentvid of Slovenia, the Hallstatt Age horses of Brezje in Krain, the Thracian horses of Bulgaria, the horses of Histria in Rumania from the sixth century B.C., as well as the Scythian and Greek horses of the Ukraine and of the south of Russia. The latter comprises the "Helvetian-Gallic" horses of Marek, the horses of La Tène, the horses of Manching and horses from some archaeological sites of the Hallstatt Age in Austria and Germany. The horses of the Hallstatt Age from Austria and Germany, only represented by some bones, along with some Manching horses can be ranged with the western group on a geographical basis only, since, due to their large measurements, they completely fall outside of this group's usual size variations which they greatly exceed. If we compare the curves of the length variations of the metapodia or of the variations of withers height of the two groups, we can see that those of the eastern group give a much more regular shape, almost that of a perfect cone and indicate only one member each that falls out of the spread in the direction of the western group. However, the curves of the western group are more irregular and are unreasonably extended toward the eastern group. The individuals to be found among the Manching horses but deviating from the size variations of the population were not considered animals of local origin by Liepe and Frank, but imported ones, most probably from Rome. However, on grounds of our present material it seems to be much more likely that these horses found their way by trade or by the events of war from the eastern group to Manching. The fact that such horses occur on archaeological sites of the Hallstatt Age in Austria or Germany also contradicts their having been imported from Rome, although if the big-bodied Manching horses had indeed been imported from Rome, this essentially would point to an eastern origin, for Roman horses along with Greek ones were subject to very strong eastern influences. Originally Greek horses must have been, like those of the western group, small-bodied animals, to prove which Vitt refers to Xenophon's advice given to a Greek horseman, viz., that having jumped on a horse he should get hold with his left hand of the highest point of the mane close by the horse's ear. But the small-bodied character of Greek horses is clearly discernible on the gold comb of the Solokha kurgan (see fig. 17), on which the withers of the Greek warrior's horse scarcely come up to the waist of the warriors standing beside him. These originally small-bodied Greek horses were subsequently improved by the great masses of horses imported from the eas-

FIG. 17. Gold comb of Soloha kurgan, with a representation of the small-bodied Greek horse.

tern group, like the twenty thousand Scythian mares imported by Philip of Macedon, or the fifty thousand eastern horses in the Persian spoil of Alexander the Great. As a result of cross-breeding with these horses the large-bodied horses of the Roman cavalry were produced, well known from the monuments of emperors but also demonstrated by Kraemer (1900) in Vindonissa, by Traininas in the

Engehalbinsel, by Gavillet in Vidy-Lausanne, by Fraas in Donnstetten, by Hilzheimer (1920; 1924) in Cannstatt, Saalburg and Zugmantel, by Amschler (1949) in Hallstatt-Lahn and by Boessneck (1957) in Cambodonum. However, it is not only the above-mentioned Austrian and German horses of the Iron Age that can be considered as imported animals from the eastern group but the horses belonging to the non-oriental people of Magdalenska gora, Šentvid and Brezje. These horses undoubtedly originate from the Scythians. This is proved by the type of Scythian bridle found in one of the Brezje graves (Kromer, 1959); several similar bridles with horses of the same type were found in the Scythian cemetery of Szentes-Vekerzug (Párducz, 1952–1955).

But let us revert again to the differences between the two groups of horses in order to be able to clarify even more the above-outlined western importation of individuals of the eastern group. In what did the two groups differ from each other? First of all there is a difference in size between the two groups, which is well reflected in the length measurements of the extremity bones and can also be realized on grounds of the values of withers heights. Out of the two groups the eastern one is the larger-bodied; its average withers height being 136.15 or 137.12 cm. respectively as demonstrated in the foregoing. The horses of the western group are considerably smaller, their average withers heights being 126.7 or 126.69 cm. respectively.

The withers height of 135.5–141 cm. of the "Helvetian-Gallic" horses as determined by Marek is exaggerated. According to Vitt the withers height of these horses but rarely comes up to 130 cm., but there are also small individuals of withers height below 120 cm. among them. Marek's exceedingly high values may be due to the fact that the author used the Nehring method when determining the withers height. According to this method the basal length is three tenths of the withers height. These horses had, like primitive horses in general, relatively big heads; we have pointed out already the extraordinary length of their facial parts.

On grounds of body size we can find here just the opposite of the Franck classification, which is based on recent horses and considers eastern horses as small-bodied and western horses as large-bodied ones. However, if we examine the slenderness relations we shall also find the opposite of the above classification. This namely evinced, though not significantly, that the metapodia of the eastern group are relatively more stocky than those of the western group, i.e., that the mountain-woodland horses have slenderer legs than the members of the steppe group. The third difference, which

for want of an adequate material of finds we only touched upon here, is manifested in certain differentiations of the characteristics of the skull, first of all with respect to the relationship between the facial and cerebral parts of the skull—this, however, requires further clarification.

On grounds of the considerable differences in body size in favor of the eastern horses, they were considered from the horsebreeder's point of view as better horses, because, owing to the greater mass of their bodies, they could carry heavier loads. With riders of the same weight they could achieve higher speeds. Also they could cover greater distances and carry armored riders more easily. These were all motives with the peoples living in territories where the horses of the western group were prevalent to acquire eastern horses which were better than their own. To achieve this was, of course, chiefly possible for distinguished personages, which is proved by the fact that in the territories mentioned above these horses were first and foremost found in graves, and only rich people such as chiefs of tribes, heads of clans, etc. were buried together with their horses. On the other hand, these horses are very rare in settlement materials, which show the entire population. By the way, these horses not only got to Europe but to Africa as well: Vitt identified a horse found in an Egyptian grave from the seventh–sixth century B.C. (Quibel-Olver, 1926) with Scythian horses on grounds of the shape of its skull, and of the manner it was placed in the grave. The skull measurements completely correspond with those of one of the masked horses of Pazyryk. The 148 cm. withers height of this horse comes up to that of the best Scythian horses.

The foundations of the eastern group are formed by Scythian horses, which moved from Northern Iran and Southern Russia, by Scythian expansion and by trade too (Minns, 1913), as far as Central Europe, North Africa and, in Asia, as far as the Altai Mountains and later with the Yakuts as far as the Arctic Ocean (Amschler, 1932). The Scythian horses of this immense territory were fairly homogeneous and even the bulk of those which got as far as the Altai Mountains show only minimal differences as against the European ones.

Fig. 18. Scenes of keeping and breaking in of horses from the electrum vase of Chertomlyk. *After* Zalkin, 1960.

The horses of the two regions do not diverge in their diagrams either. Concerning these differences Zalkin (1952) and Vitt state that the changes in question are only due to unfavorable conditions of the environs. On most different works of art and objects of everyday use of the Scythian period, innumerable representations of the Scythian horse are to be found. However, the best representations of the average Scythian horse are on the electrum vase of the fourth century B.C. of the kurgan of Chertomlyk in the Ukraine (fig. 18 after Zalkin). The frieze of this vase shows scenes of the keeping and breaking in of horses in representations most true to life. The horses depicted there can be considered thoroughbreds even by today's horse breeders' standards. They are mostly reminiscent of Arab thoroughbreds with relatively small heads and concave profiles, with tails held like banners. The latter point is characteristic of Arab thoroughbreds even today. However they also differ from them in certain features, especially in thick and stocky necks and bodies. A part of these horses are short-maned, which, however, does not necessarily mean that they are wild, although in the territory of the Ukraine and of Southern Russia there were wild horses to be found until the beginning of the nineteenth century. From the very time of the Scythians Herodotus made mention of white

wild horses from the region of the Hypanis River, today's Bug in the south of the Ukraine, which were identified both by Vetulani (1952, 1954) and by ourselves with the tarpan. One of the short-maned horses on the Chertomlyk vase has a bridle and a saddle, the latter being one of the earliest representations of a saddle, and testifies to a highly developed form of riding. By the way, the masked horses in the kurgans of Pazyryk also have saddles, and most of the horse mummies of the Pazyryk kurgans have manes cropped short. We have studied at the Institute of Zoology in Leningrad as well as at the Hermitage three horse mummies from Pazyryk, and their manes too were cropped short. The custom of the Scythians of cutting their horses' manes short is attributed by Vitt to the circumstance that their archers would have been hindered in handling their weapons by the horses' long manes. The fact that the horses of the Chertomlyk vase were larger-bodied than the Greek horses is evident if we compare them with the figures of men standing beside them. The withers of the horses come up to the chests of the men and even to the shoulders of the slave (?) whose hand is cut off, which refers to withers heights of 140 cm. at least. The representation of the hunting horseman of Kul Oba, too, (Minns, 1913) shows a large-bodied horse, the rider's foot being at least half a meter's distance from the ground, whereas the foot of the Greek rider of Soloha almost reaches the ground. The shapes of the Scythian horses that found their way to the Altaian region are still preserved by the modern Mongolian horses, with their short and broad heads (figs. 19,20).

The representations of the Chertomlyk vase show the average Scythian horse that can be found at Szentes-Vekerzug and in the settlements of Southern Russia alike and that supplied the majority of the horses of the Altaian kurgans. However, in every grave of the Altaian kurgans and, in our opinion, now and then in the Scythian material of the south of Russia, there were certain horses whose size exceeded that of the average. In his study Vitt generally ranges these horses of outstanding size in the same group as the former. Sometimes, however, he considers them to be members of an independent group of a special Central Asian origin. Anyhow, it seems that, side by side with the undoubtedly excellent Scythian horses, there existed in Central Asia smaller local groups of horses. The members of these groups were larger of body and perhaps also possessed other eminent qualities lacking in the former. They must have been valued highly by the Scythians themselves, and so it was only the leaders who came by them—and even they could only acquire few of them—since only one was found in each kurgan. Chinese sources, too, made mention of these horses (Yetts, Huppertz, 1962). The horses in question were chiefly Ferghana horses, whose fame was well known in China too. The Chinese waged several wars to acquire these horses and sometimes captured three thousand of them, or, in case of their victory, levied regular taxes to be paid in horses. These sources point out that the horses in question were slender and big as against the Chinese ones. In the excellent horses of the kurgans of Pazyryk, Vitt seems to have found this group, and demonstrated this fact on an osteological basis too. Evidently these horses had played a part in developing Persian horses, which, according to several sources were so very excellent. Unfortunately, for want of finds we do not know anything of the latter from the point of view of osteology but hope that excavations of the near future will present us with richer materials.

The strikingly large individuals of our diagrams are provided by these horses. Besides, as already mentioned, Vitt considered it highly probable that these horses had been geldings, expounding that due to the fact that their extremity bones continue to grow for a longer time, the geldings of the same breed are taller by about four to six cm. than the stallions or mares. This is exactly the difference that divides this group of horses of the kurgans of Pazyryk from the rest of the horses. However, Vitt's hypothesis can hardly stand on its own if we consider that the method of determining withers height on grounds of the extremity bones used by Vitt sets arbitrary limits between the groups of sizes. The fact that in our diagrams these horses do not form a definitely independent group also contradicts Vitt's assumptions and so does their extraordinary variability on grounds of the slenderness index. Vitt, by the way, did not state in his paper what he had observed from this point of view on the mummified horses, a number of which he had had the opportunity of inspecting. This group of horses, by the way, was only found now and then in Eastern Europe in some archaeological sites of Southern Russia and in Histria in Rumania but had never reached Central Europe. On rock drawings of Central Asia its representations have been found since we think it probable that the rock drawings published by Bernstam and Zadneprovsky depict these horses (fig. 21).

Very little is known about the horses of the western group as against those of the eastern one, and we think this is due to a number of reasons:

1. The circumstance is doubtless of primary importance that in the western part of Central Europe and in Western Europe, the Bronze Age, which marks the beginnings of horse-keeping,[1] did not represent in duration and significance a period of equal importance with that of the territories where the eastern group was prevailing. Accordingly, with respect to

[1] I am not sure that neolithic horses were domesticated. Domestication of the horse probably began in the Calcolithic or Copper Age. By this I mean the domestication of horses born wild. True horse-keeping, the rearing of horses in captivity as domestic animals, only began in the Bronze Age.

Fig. 19. Short- and broad-headed Mongolian horse.

Fig. 20. Short- and broad-headed Mongolian horses.

FIG. 21. Rock drawings from the Altai. *After* Zadneprovsky.

the former territory our information about the immediate predecessors of the horses of the Iron Age is rather incomplete.

2. The second reason is that although the horse played a great part in the lives of certain peoples of Central and Western Europe, thus e.g., in the lives of the Celts, its significance and its numerical proportion within the live-stock strongly fell behind the role it played in the lives of the nomadic equestrian peoples and in their livestock respectively. Hence horse bones did not occur in so great numbers in western settlements and cemeteries as in the territories of the eastern group. Practically this meant that their study in a suitable manner was impossible. In Central and Western Europe, there are no graves to be found from any peri-od of the Iron Age with so great a number of

horses buried in them as in the kurgans of Eastern Europe or Central Asia.

3. Another reason, and not an insignificant one, is the fact that in the western territories the archaeological sites of the Iron Age, and particularly of the late Iron Age, had a contin-uation of life in the Roman Age. Thus, in most cases, the material of the two periods was col-lected together, and hence the Iron Age ma-terial could not be evaluated separately.

4. The territory of the western group lacks such lucky finds as the Pazyryk ones, where, owing to advantageous geological and climatic conditions, the material was saved from de-composition and would give us a clue from which conclusions could be drawn as to the formation of the hair, the hooves, the soft parts, etc., to the color and irregularities of the hair

and hooves and the general condition of the animals.

5. Finally, in the territory of the western group, written history commenced somewhat later and thus we do not possess the same number of written sources as in the case of the territories of Southern Russia or Central Asia about the horses of which Greek and Chinese sources respectively reported.

Among the horses of this group particularly little is known about those of the Hallstatt Age; nor do the results of our present material of investigation especially increase our knowledge, since the material of the Hallstatt Age elaborated here was insignificantly little. About the horses of the La Tène period, the second part of the Iron Age, however, somewhat more can be reported since the overwhelming majority of the western material elaborated here originated from that period.

First of all we must destroy the romantic hypothesis, which originated at the end of the last century but here and there is still alive, that the Celts were the best horse-breeders of the Iron Age and their horses the best individuals of the period. This assumption, by the way, was already refuted by Boessneck (1958) when he demonstrated that the Celtic horses were to be considered as the lowest link in a process of diminishing body-size; the smallest-bodied horses at the end of the chain. Now it has turned out that parallel with the Celtic horses there lived a group of horses in the eastern part of Central Europe, in Southeast and Eastern Europe whose members were larger of body than the Celtic horses. As will be seen from the following, the Celts are not to be blamed at all for these differences which were not due to their defective knowledge of breeding, the more so as the Celts only kept horses but did not pursue rational breeding. They did not practice breeding selection, so they could not be expected to breed some race better than those surrounding them. Nevertheless, a significant chapter of the European history of the horse began with the Celts' keeping horses: equestrian traditions of Western Europe originated with the Celts (Hartenstein). With them horses were highly appreciated and even found their way into their mythology; the cult of Epona the goddess of fertility probably originated from the cult of a horse deity. The goddess herself was often represented mounted on horseback, surrounded by mares in foal, and by horses or asses. The horse may possibly have been a kind of totem-animal with the Celts and was highly important among them. Other domestic animals like the bull and the pig also played the role of totem-animals with them. This is shown by the frequency of representations of the horse to be found both on coins and on tombstones; representations which are often rather stylized, particularly on coins, but often very realistic and demonstrate quite well the characteristic features of Celtic horses, the long facial part of the skull and the small body measurements. Such are the horses' heads on the porticus of Roquepertuse, which have very long facial parts (see fig. 22, after Moreau) and the small-bodied horses represented on the Gundestrup cauldron (see fig. 23, *after* Moreau).

The larger body measurements of the horses of the eastern group can be traced back to several causes. One of them is that, although the domestic horse is a very plastic species and can well adapt itself to the most varied conditions of the environs, it was originally the animal of the steppe or of steppe forest. Thus it is evident that on the steppes of Eastern Europe and of Central Asia where the life conditions were ideal, populations of larger bodies got developed than in the mountainous and forest-clad territories where the western group lived. Under the circumstances of primitive livestock-keeping, the different conditions of the climate, the soil, the food and the way of living in the several areas may produce local "breeds." These cannot be considered as genuine breeds, for they did not appear as a result of man's conscious breeding activity. We consider them only as local groups whose different qualities, like, e.g., the size of their bodies, are due, in addition to the above-mentioned reasons, also to other factors like a relatively earlier or later domestication, or to their origin from different local groups or perhaps subspecies of the common wild ancestor. If some of the individuals of such a local group find their way to another area it may happen that they strongly differ from the horses that live in the new place and have possibly formed a local group there. In such cases the researcher may get the impression that two breeds were living in the same

Fig. 22. Horses' heads from the Celtic porticus of Roquepertuse. *After* Moreau.

Fig. 23. Representation of small-bodied Celtic horses on the Gundestrup cauldron. *After* Moreau.

territory simultaneously. Such was the case, e.g., with the cattle of the Neolithic Age in Hungary. It seemed that a few, small-bodied individuals had formed an independent breed, different from the majority of cattle. However, these can only be considered as cattle imported from another territory, most probably from the Balkan Peninsula, cattle which had had a long past of domestication and had got much smaller than cattle in Hungary (Bökönyi - Kubasiewicz). Such a group may be the case with the eastern horses, a group and not a breed, which, owing to better conditions of living grew to a larger size, whereas the horses of the western group of the same period, constituted a group that had become smaller of body due to the less suitable local conditions.

As another reason we may mention the probability of breeding selection having emerged in the territories of Eastern Europe and Central Asia, and by dint of this, the very beginnings of planned livestock breeding in a certain sense, there resulted horses larger of body. According to opinions prevailing today in the science of domestic animals, there was no breeding selection or planned livestock-breeding prior to Roman times (Herre, 1958). We do not consider it impossible to assume that in Central Asia, where horse-keeping is rooted most deeply (obviously the earliest domestication, the nomadic way of life of nations of horsemen, etc.) side by side with a high standard of horse-keeping, the rudimentary forms of horse-breeding got developed as early as in the Iron Age. The principal criterion of planned breeding, i.e., the application of breeding selection, would be hard to prove by the very nature of things. However, our view is strongly supported by two factors. One is the circumstance that in the kurgans of Pazyryk there were two types of horses to be found, different in constitution and in size. Their manner of keeping, of feeding and of harnessing was different, and so was apparently the way in which they were put to use. The other is the fact that according to Chinese sources as early as the first centuries B.C. the emperors of China introduced a compulsory examination of mares and the setting up of stud-farms (Yetts, Huppertz, 1962). However, the Chinese took over the high standards of horse-keeping as well as their very best horses

from the nomads of Central Asia, and it is to be suspected that along with the excellent horses they adopted the methods of horse-keeping and probably also of horse-breeding of those nomadic people too. Thus, if the rudiments of horse-breeding could be found with the Chinese in the first centuries B.C., it seems to be likely that the same activities were started by the nomadic peoples of Central Asia even sooner.

Differences of origin may also have played a part in the emergence of size differences between the two groups, but for the time being we do not wish to go into them in detail. However, we consider further investigations to be necessary in order to decide whether the horses of the western group originated from an eastern center of domestication and were introduced into the western part of Central Europe already in a domesticated form, and whether it was there that due to unfavorable conditions of the soil and the climate, or possibly due to the way they were kept, they got smaller; or whether they originated from other, perhaps smaller-bodied, Western European wild forms or subspecies which were different from the wild horses of Eastern Europe and Asia. It would be well worth while to compare our material of the Iron Age horses of the eastern group with the Bronze Age and Neolithic horses of Central Europe. But one thing is beyond doubt, viz., that, in spite of the fact that the western group is chiefly represented in our material by the horses of the second period of the Iron Age, i.e., by the La Tène period, the difference in size between the two groups cannot be the result of the process of shrinking which according to Nobis (1955) lasted until the Hallstatt Age and according to Boessneck (1958) until the La Tène period, since there are horses frequently to be found in the eastern groups which were unearthed in archaeological sites of southern Russia and which essentially correspond with the Western European La Tène period in their age (e.g., Geroyevka and Kamenskoye: fifth to second centuries B.C.; Gavrilovskoye from the second century B.C. to the first A.D., etc.). And yet these horses are bigger than the individuals of the western group. Even a fleeting examination of the Bronze Age horses of Central and Eastern Europe showed that these horses formed a fairly homogeneous group and no local sub-groups could be discerned among them. This points to the fact that a domestication of any importance could only exist in Eastern Europe, and that in the Bronze Age the body sizes of western horses were identical with those of the eastern ones because there had not been enough time for them to become smaller due to the worse climatic and soil conditions. This process of diminishing in size only took place in later periods and reached its peak in the Iron Age. It seems to be most probable therefore that the two European groups of horses of the Iron Age described in the foregoing were of the same origin and were divided and developed only due to the different conditions of their environments.

CHAPTER VI

PATHOLOGICAL LESIONS

AS OBSERVED earlier, pathological lesions were not infrequent on the skeletons of horses from Scythian burials. Thus Zalkin (1952) in each case found pathological lesions on the horses of the Altaian kurgans he examined; first of all deformations of the hoof-bone and exostoses on the extremity bones. On the extremity bones of the Scythian horses of Szentes-Vekerzug in two or maybe three cases lesions could be found from which the lameness of the animals could be inferred (Bökönyi, 1954, 1955). Vitt, too, found such symptoms but he did not go into details, only mentioned the wrinkles on the horny walls of the hooves, which, as he pointed out, were to be found on every horse of Pazyryk, with the exception of the masked ones, and which testified to the grave winter starvation the animals must have undergone.

Many pathological deformations of the bones were described by Liepe, Boessneck-Dahne as well as by Frank who found them on the Manching horses. These lesions appeared in the first line on the tarsus in the form of arthropathia chronica deformans et ankylopoetica and in one case on the proximal end of a humerus in the form of periostitis ossificans.

In the material published here for the first time there were some pathological lesions to be found on the horse skeletons of Magdalenska gora and Stična (Šentvid). These lesions can be divided into three groups:

1. lesions of the teeth,
2. lesions of the vertebrae,
3. lesions of the extremity bones.

1. Out of the three groups enumerated above, the pathological lesions of the teeth are the most frequent, but, at the same time, they are the mildest ones. They are the following:

a. A very strong incrustation of tartar particularly on the buccal side can be observed on horses I and II of the 29th grave of tumulus No. V at Magdalenska gora as well as on the horse-tooth found in the 18th grave of tumulus No. X at the same place, and also on the horse found in the 47th grave of the Trondel tumulus (Tumulus IV) at Šentvid, one of the cemeteries of Stična.

b. A mild and wavy attrition can be seen on the horse found in the fifth grave of the tumulus No. V at Magdalenska gora. This is due to the difference in hardness in different parts of the substance of the teeth.

c. In the 29th grave of tumulus No. V at Magdalenska gora the oral part of the upper and lower P_1-s had been abraded almost to the root in horse No. II; in horse No. I the chewing surface of the lower P_1-s was abraded by 4-5 mm. Here the upper P_1-s were not collected. The oral parts of the P_1-s frame the diastema, and when the reins are pulled, the bit of the bridle presses against these parts. With the same parts of its teeth the animal also chews the bit. So the above phenomenon was caused by the abrasive effect of the bridle. Horse No. I having been an old animal, the attrition caused on its teeth by the bridle is stronger, whereas horse No. II having been a younger animal, the attrition on its teeth was of a smaller degree (see fig. 21).

d. On horse No. I of the 29th grave of tumulus No. V at Magdalenska gora some small excrescences of bone can be seen on the ventral side of the mandible. Most probably these are in causal relation with the harnessing. The predecessors of metal bridles, the bridles of bones and antlers are proved to have been twisting bridles[1] (Bökönyi, 1953); the same refers to the early bronze and iron bridles too.

[1] These bone and antler bits have a hole toward one end for one of the reins. When this rein was pulled, the bit was twisted in the horse's mouth. This at the same time tightened the strap under the horse's lower jaw that held the bit in place. This could cause pain and over a long period of time bony excrescences on the jawbone as well. The bit in Tumulus V, grave 29, is not identical with the bone and antler ones, but it is similar, and one pair of reins could be used for a twisting effect that would tighten the strap in the same way under the lower jaw.

When the reins are pulled, the strap of the bridle under the chin presses against the ventral side of the mandible and hurts the animal at that point too; thus its curbing effect is greater. On old animals, like the above horse, the above-mentioned exostoses could easily develop as a result of the mechanical irritation often repeated during a long period.

2. On the Magdalenska gora material the gravest pathological lesions are to be found on the vertebrae and again on the aforesaid old horse. These lesions extend over the nine last thoracic and the first two lumbar vertebrae. It is not impossible that they appeared on some more thoracic and lumbar vertebrae as well, these however have not been collected. Essentially, the lesions are the following: on the corpus of the vertebrae, but first of all on their arcus and small joints there are huge exostoses, which rigidly join the vertebrae (fig. 2). The exostoses are the biggest on the lumbar vertebrae, they completely cover them; on the last thoracic vertebrae they are somewhat weaker and look like laths; they chiefly extend over the small joints and the ventral part of the vertebral corpus and thus the dorsal part of the caput craniale is left free. The most cranially situated impaired thoracic vertebra shows much milder symptoms; on it exostoses can mainly be found on the caudoventral part of the vertebral corpus. It can be stated that the process proceeded in a cranial direction. It started on the lumbar vertebrae and slowly proceeded toward the upper segments of the vetebral column. Thus it is not impossible that a particularly grave case of the Behterew disease must have taken place here. Unfortunately, we cannot declare anything with full certainty in this respect; to be able to do so we should need a closer x-ray examination of the parts in question of the vertebral column. One thing is sure: the disease doubtlessly brought about grave disorders of motion with the animal, which could by no means have been used as a mount and hardly as a draught animal.

3. The lesions of the extremity bones are also to be found on the skeleton of the same old horse.

a. On both metacarpals it can be observed that the side metacarpals (mc_2 and mc_4) are grown on to the main piece. On old animals this is an almost physiological phenomenon, which does not cause any disorders of motion.

b. In about the middle of the left side metacarpal, on the dorsal surface there is a slightly protruding and mildly rough exostosis (spavin). This deformity, which is also a concomitant of old age and of hard work, can cause lameness even in so mild a form.

The above lesions indicate three things: 1) the lesions of the teeth are mostly insignificant ones; the only important lesion, the attrition of the oral side of the P_1-s was caused by the bridle. 2) The horses must have been taxed to the utmost; they had to draw heavy loads or carry heavy riders, perhaps on very bad ground. These circumstances caused pathological lesions—sometimes such as resulted in disturbances of motion—on horses which grew old. 3) As both Zalkin (1952) and we ourselves (1954) pointed out, viz., that weakened, diseased and lame individuals were chosen to be placed beside the dead is a fact proved here too. This is a phenomenon not uninteresting from an archaeological point of view and as such shows the growing obsolescence of a funeral rite, which still lived in its form but had lost its content. Good parallels for this can be found in the graves with horses in Hungary of the Avars of sixth to ninth century A.D. and of the Magyars of the time of the Conquest, ninth to tenth century A.D., in which most of the skeletons of horses show pathological lesions, generally lameness. On these grounds one may assume that the other horses found in the graves whose bones do not display any pathological lesions must have suffered from some other disease and therefore were laid beside the dead in the grave.

Chapter VII

SUMMARY

THE IRON Age horses of Central and Eastern Europe can be divided into two groups, which can be separated also according to the areas where they lived. One, the eastern group, can be traced back to the Scythian horses and as such followed up in Asia as far as the Altai Mountains; in Eastern Europe and the eastern part of Central Europe up to the line of Vienna-Venice it was the only prevalent group. The other, the western group, on the other hand belongs to the Iron Age in the western part of Central Europe and occurred in its most characteristic form as the horse of the Celts. Out of the two groups the eastern horses were bigger of body and better from a breeder's point of view. It was for this very characteristic that they found their way from the Scythians to other peoples too. Examples are the horses belonging to this type found at Magdalenska gora, Stična (Šentvid) and Brezje and the big-bodied horses now and then found on Celtic sites. It is also evident that they played a part in the development of the big-bodied Roman horse too. Thus, with respect to the size of the body, we have gained a picture absolutely contrasting with the old notions; but we have also gained a contrasting picture regarding the slenderness of the horses: the small-bodied, woodland and mountain horses of the western group had slenderer legs than the big-bodied steppe horses belonging to the eastern group. It seems to be highly probable that the differences between the two groups were due to the differences in climatic and soil conditions and perhaps to the different ways in which they were kept; the horses of the Bronze Age all over Europe, the ancestors of the Iron Age horses of the western part of the continent, show on grounds of material available up to now, a homogeneous picture, and this seems to contradict the idea that they were of different origins, though they may have come originally from the steppes of Eastern Europe or Asia (see p. 8). As for the Iron Age horses of Eastern Europe, they came at a later time from northwestern Asia.

MEASUREMENTS

Skull

	Tápiószele grave 145	Magdalenska gora Tumulus IV, grave 43	Brezje Tumulus VI, grave 1–2
1. Basal length	473*	—	—
2. From the oral part of M_1 to prosthion	209	—	—
3. From the oral part of M_1 to basion		—	—
4. From basion to the aboral part of palate		—	—
5. Length of palate	244	—	—
6. From prosthion to the lateral part of os temporale	408	—	—
7. From prosthion to the point where the connecting line of aboral ends of ossa nasalia crosses the median suture	325	—	—
8. From prosthion to the point where the connecting line of the most lateral parts of ossa frontalia crosses the median suture	369	—	—
9. From prosthion to foramen infraorbitale	214	—	—
10. Dental length from prosthion to aboral part of M_3	291	—	—
11. Length of incisor row	14	—	—
12. Length of diastema	101	—	—
13. $P_1 — P_3$	82	—	94
14. $M_1 — M_3$	72	—	80
15. Frontal breadth	205	—	—
16. Distance between the medial borders of orbits	140	—	—
17. Distance between foramina supraorbitalia	146	135	—
18. Distance between the oral ends of both cristae faciales	147	—	—
19. Distance between foramina infraorbitalia	76	—	—
20. $P_1 — P_1$	98	—	—
21. $M_1 — M_1$	116	—	—
22. Meatus acusticus-breadth	120*	—	—
23. Distance between processus jugulares	—	—	108
24. Distance between condyli occipitales	—	—	81
25. Distance between jaw articulations	193	—	—
26. Greatest breadth of brain case	107	—	—
27. Length of foramen magnum	—	—	34
28. Breadth of foramen magnum	—	—	34
29. Horizontal diameter of orbits	63	—	—
30. Vertical diameter of orbits	56	—	—
31. Breadth of incisor row	69	—	—
32. Breadth over canines	63	—	—

* = approximately

Mandible

	Magdalenska gora Tumulus V, grave 29		Brezje Tumulus VI, grave 1–2	
	horse I	horse II	horse I	horse II
1. Height to articular process	—	—	—	—
2. Height before P_1	55.5	—	—	50.5
3. Height before M_1	73.5	—	92	72
4. $P_1 — P_3$	78	92	92	82
5. $M_1 — M_3$	75	83.5	85	79

Atlas

	Magdalenska gora Tumulus V, grave 29		Brezje Tumulus VI, grave 1–2	
	horse I	horse II	horse I	horse II
1. Length of corpus	36.5	35.5	36.5	—
2. Length of arcus	42	37	41	—
3. Length of wings	—	—	—	87
4. Breadth of cranial articulation	83	82	82	78
5. Breadth of caudal articulation	83.5	—	81.5	79
6. Greatest height	—	—	75	—

Axis

	Magdalenska gora Tumulus V, grave 29 horse II	Brezje Tumulus VI, grave 1–2 horse I
1. Length of corpus	140	—
2. Length of dens	22	19
3. Breadth of cranial articulation	78	76
4. Breadth of dens	34	39
5. Depth of cranial articulation	43	38
6. Breadth of caudal articulation	—	38
7. Greatest breadth	—	82

Scapula

	Breadth of collum	Breadth of distal end	Breadth of articular surface
Magdalenska gora Tumulus V, grave 29, Horse I	62.5	90	—
Magdalenska gora Tumulus V, grave 29, Horse II	85*	—	—
Stična (Šentvid) Tumulus IV, grave 16	61	87*	45*
Szentes-Vekerzug, grave 6 or 8	—	90*	42*

* = approximately

Humerus

	Greatest length	Breadth of the proximal end	Minimum breadth	Breadth of the distal end	Depth of the proximal end	Minimum depth	Depth of the distal end
Magdalenska gora							
Tumulus V, grave 29, Horse I	280*	87	30	70*	92	39	76
Tumulus V, grave 29, Horse I	280*	—	30	73	—	38	79
Tumulus V, grave 29, Horse II	263*	—	31	72*	95*	38	—
Tumulus V, grave 29, Horse II	262*	—	31	72	—	35	80
Brezje							
Tumulus VI, grave 1-2, Horse I	—	—	41	76	—	45	77
Szentes-Vekerzug							
Grave 6 or 8	270	87	31	71	—	39	75
Grave 6 or 8	270	89	32	—	96	40	—
Neapol skijski (South Russia)	315	103	37	82	—	—	—
	312	98	36	85	—	—	—
	293	94	37	81	—	—	—
	288	92	38	78	—	—	—
	287	97	37	83	—	—	—
	286	—	36	78	—	—	—
	278	—	36	76	—	—	—

Radius

	Greatest length	Breadth of the proximal end	Minimum breadth	Breadth of the distal end	Depth of the proximal end	Minimum depth	Depth of the distal end
Magdalenska gora							
Tumulus V, grave 29, Horse I	332*	—	34	73	44	24	43
Tumulus V, grave 29, Horse I	332*	80	34	73	42.5	24	44
Tumulus V, grave 29, Horse II	313	79*	34	69	42	23	42
Tumulus V, grave 29, Horse II	—	79	34	—	41	23	—
Brezje							
Tumulus VI, grave 1-2, Horse I	335*	—	41	75	46	31	43.5
Tumulus VI, grave 1-2, Horse I	335*	78	41	—	46	30.5	44
Szentes-Vekerzug							
Grave 6 or 8	320*	77	36	69	44.5	29	39
Grave 6 or 8	320*	78	—	67	44	—	39
Velemszentvid							
S. M. number: 54.448.1	—	78	34.5	73.5	43.5	24.5	46
S. M. number: 54.484.1	330	78	—	—	45.5	—	—
S. M. number: 54.484.2	—	—	—	68	—	—	39.5
S. M. number: 54.484.3	345*	82.5	36.5	—	46.5	28	—
South-Russian finds:							
Neapol skifski	375	85	42	84	—	—	—
	331	80	40	75	—	—	—
	320	80	40	—	—	—	—
	319	84	40	74	—	—	—
	318	82	39	76	—	—	—
Olbia	344	—	41.5	76.3	—	—	—
	325	78	39.2	74.5	—	—	—
	328	79.8	37.9	72.6	—	—	—
	307	74.3	38.2	69.6	—	—	—
Pantikapei	321	—	41	75	—	—	—
Mirmekii	325	83	43	78	—	—	—
	370	80	39	78	—	—	—
	365	81	41	79	—	—	—
	314	81	37.5	76	—	—	—
	322	—	38	—	—	—	—
Germonassa	318	—	38	—	—	—	—

* = approximately

Metacarpus

	Greatest length	Breadth of the proximal end	Minimum breadth	Breadth of the distal end	Depth of the proximal end	Minimum depth	Depth of the distal end
Magdalenska gora							
Tumulus IV, grave 43	211	46	30	—	31	20	—
Tumulus IV, grave 43	212*	47*	30	—	—	20	—
Tumulus V, grave 29, Horse I	219	49	32	46.5	34	22	36
Tumulus V, grave 29, Horse I	219.5	48*	31.5	47*	35	22	36
Tumulus V, grave 29, Horse II	214.5	48*	30	—	—	20.5	—
Tumulus V, grave 29, Horse II	214.5	48*	30.5	—	—	21	—
Brezje							
Tumulus VI, grave 1-2, Horse I	—	50	—	—	33.5	—	—
Szentes-Vekerzug							
Grave 6 or 8	210	44.5	32	46	33.5	21.5	—
Grave 6 or 8	210*	45	32	46.5	33.5	21.5	—
Histria							
Number P. 1	230	53	35	50.5	34	23	36
Number P. 2	235	53.2	34	50	34	24	39
Number P. 3	221*	—	33	—	—	21	—
Number P. 4	229	51	32.1	—	32	22	—
Number P. 12	225	50	34	51	33	23.3	37
South-Russian finds:							
Neapol skifski	245	54	35	54	—	—	—
	244	57	36	56	—	—	—
	244	57	36	56	—	—	—
	243	55	36	57	—	—	—
	241	54	37	53	—	—	—
	240	54	36	54	—	—	—
	238	52	36	53	—	—	—
	235	53	37	51.5	—	—	—
	233	—	37	51	—	—	—
	225	—	36	—	—	—	—
	224	53	36	53	—	—	—
	224	53	36	53	—	—	—
	221	—	33	50	—	—	—
	220	50	36	48	—	—	—
	219	50	33	—	—	—	—
	219	48	33	49	—	—	—
	219	49	34	47	—	—	—
	218	49	34	48	—	—	—
	217	50	35	—	—	—	—
	216	50	36	48	—	—	—
	216	47	32	46	—	—	—
	208	48.5	34	—	—	—	—
	229	48	30.5	50	—	—	—
Peresadowskoe gorodišče	231	53	30.5	49.6	—	—	—
	221	—	34.5	50.5	—	—	—
Kamenskoe gorodišče	225	51	37	51.5	—	—	—
	225	50	34.5	49	—	—	—
	215	48	33.5	47	—	—	—
	226	50	34	52	—	—	—
	215	50	33.5	49	—	—	—
	212	45	30	45	—	—	—
	211	48	30	47	—	—	—
	210	47	30	44	—	—	—
	220	48.5	33	47.5	—	—	—
	225	52	37	52	—	—	—
	222	50	36.5	53	—	—	—
	213	—	33	51	—	—	—
	221	—	—	49.5	—	—	—

	Greatest length	Breadth of the proximal end	Minimum breadth	Breadth of the distal end	Depth of the proximal end	Minimum depth	Depth of the distal end
Olbia	229	52	36	49	—	—	—
	228	52	34.5	—	—	—	—
	223	52	34	52	—	—	—
	221	49	34	—	—	—	—
	205	43	32	44	—	—	—
	216	50	32	49	—	—	—
	222	50	32.5	52	—	—	—
	222	—	34.5	50	—	—	—
	231	50	33	51	—	—	—
	221	49	30.5	48	—	—	—
	215	51.5	39	50	—	—	—
Semenowka	199	45	30	43	—	—	—
Ilupat	198	46	29	45	—	—	—
Germonassa	226	51	33	50	—	—	—
	216	47	33.5	47	—	—	—
	229	49	32.5	—	—	—	—
	230	51	37.5	50	—	—	—
	213	48	32	47	—	—	—
	212	46	32	46	—	—	—
Kery	213	48	32	47	—	—	—
	212	46	32	46	—	—	—
Feodosia	226	48	32	48	—	—	—
	226	49.5	48	32.5	—	—	—
Sasonowka	229	52	32.5	49	—	—	—
	229	49	33	48.5	—	—	—
Suiur-Tash	222	50.5	32.5	50.5	—	—	—
Fanagoria	218	51	36	47	—	—	—
	225	50	31	47	—	—	—
	218	47.5	32.5	46.5	—	—	—
Semidratnee gorodišče	228	52	33.5	—	—	—	—
Tanais	226	—	33	48	—	—	—
	220	48	33	48	—	—	—
	214	51	34.5	50	—	—	—
	219	49	32.5	49	—	—	—
	212	—	31	46	—	—	—
	210	47	32.5	47	—	—	—
	217	50	35	49	—	—	—
	218	48	32.5	—	—	—	—
	223	54	34	—	—	—	—
	227	55	35	51	—	—	—
	221	46	31	45	—	—	—
Pantikapei	222	48	34.5	48	—	—	—
	216	51	35.5	50	—	—	—
	209	51	35	48	—	—	—
	206	47	31.5	45	—	—	—
	207	49	32	48	—	—	—
	219	51	36	50	—	—	—
	214	50	31.5	48	—	—	—
	219	51	36	50	—	—	—
	217	47	32	47	—	—	—
	220	—	37	51	—	—	—
	216	48	34	46	—	—	—
	227	49	33.5	50	—	—	—
	217	47	34	47	—	—	—
	230	50	32.5	—	—	—	—
	230	51	38	50	—	—	—

	Greatest length	Breadth of the proximal end	Minimum breadth	Breadth of the distal end	Depth of the proximal end	Minimum depth	Depth of the distal end
Mirmekii	227	52	33	52	—	—	—
	231	51	35	51	—	—	—
	228	50	35	51	—	—	—
	233	52	36	54	—	—	—
	223	50	33	47	—	—	—
	229	50	35	51	—	—	—
	226	49	32.5	47	—	—	—
	218	49	34	50	—	—	—
	217	—	34	51	—	—	—
	221	49	30	48	—	—	—
	214	50	30	51	—	—	—
	222	50	34.5	51	—	—	—
	223	51	35	51	—	—	—
Finds from kurgans of Altai							
Pazyryk	227.5	49	33	50	35.5	23	37.5
	225	51	33.5	49.5	37	23.5	36
	226	52	34	40.5	35.5	23.5	38
	206	49	33	48*	32.5	20	35
	209	45	32	44.5	33	20	32.5
Other kurgans	223	51	35	52.5	36	23.5	37.5
	235	54.5	36	51.5	34	24	36
	236	50.5	33	50.5	36	23	37.5
	211.5	47	31.5	45.5	35	21	35
	233	52	35	50.5	37	25	38
	231.5	52.5	37	52	37	22.5	37
	226	50	33	49.5	38	21	38
	222	52.5	34.5	50.5	37.5	23.5	37.5
	226	53.5	34	50	36.5	22	38
	236	56	37.5	55.5	40	25	40.5

Femur

	Greatest length	Breadth of the proximal end	Minimum breadth	Breadth of the distal end	Depth of the proximal end	Minimum depth	Depth of the distal end
Magdalenska gora							
Tumulus V, grave 29, Horse I	380*	105	36.5	86	79	44	—
Tumulus V, grave 29, Horse II	367*	—	32	88*	92	42	114*
Tumulus V, grave 29, Horse II	367*	—	32.5	89*	—	42	—
Tumulus V, grave 29, Horse III	—	—	—	85*	—	—	113*
Brezje							
Tumulus VI, grave 1-2, Horse I	—	107	38	—	80	46	—
Tumulus VI, grave 1-2, Horse I	—	—	38	81	—	44	117
Szentes-Vekerzug							
Grave 6 or 8	—	—	35	—	—	45.5	—

Tibia

	Greatest length	Breadth of the proximal end	Minimum breadth	Breadth of the distal end	Depth of the proximal end	Minimum depth	Depth of the distal end
Magdalenska gora							
Tumulus V, grave 29, Horse I	342*	88*	34	65	84	27.5	43
Tumulus V, grave 29, Horse I	342*	87*	34	—	83	27.5	42.5
Tumulus V, grave 29, Horse II	335*	—	33.5	64	—	25.5	38*
Tumulus V, grave 29, Horse II	335*	—	33.5	—	—	25.5	40*
Tumulus V, grave 29, Horse III	335*	—	36	68*	83*	26	45
Tumulus V, grave 29, Horse III	—	—	36	67	—	25	43*
Tumulus V, grave 29, Horse IV	—	—	36.5	—	—	28.5	—
Stična (Šentvid)							
Tumulus Trondel, grave 47	—	—	36.5	—	—	27	—
Szentes-Vekerzug							
Grave 6 or 8	341	—	37	64.5	95	29	41.5
Grave 6 or 8	340	—	38.5	—	—	28.5	42.5
Velemszentvid							
S. M. number: 54.494.1.	352*	—	43	72.5	—	32	46
S. M. number: 54.494.2.	356	94	38.5	73	—	30.5	48.5
South-Russian finds:							
Neapol skifski							
	342	96	40	71	87	—	45
	344	93	42	71	—	—	42
	344	—	39.5	71	—	—	43
	345	—	40	71	—	—	43
Kamenskoe gorodišče							
	343	—	43	73	—	—	43
	337	87	38	70	80	—	43
Olbia							
	343	—	40	73	—	—	44
	339.5	95	38	73	85	—	45
	350	93	44	72	—	—	44
	336	—	41	72	84	—	44
	334	—	39.5	—	83	—	43
	328	—	35	67	—	—	43
Pantikapei							
	353	95	38.5	69	82	—	—
Mirmekii							
	380	95	42.5	75	86	—	43.5
	375	94	41.5	73.	83	—	42
	360	—	44	76	—	—	47
	345	—	41	73	—	—	44.5
	347	—	43	72	—	—	43.5
Tanais							
	334	95	39	73	83	—	45

* = approximately

Astragalus	Greatest length	Greatest breadth	Greatest depth
Magdalenska gora			
Tumulus V, grave 29, Horse I	60	58	57
Tumulus V, grave 29, Horse III	57	61	50
Szentes-Vekerzug			
Grave 6 or 8	57	59	53
Grave 6 or 8	—	—	54

Calcaneus	Greatest length	Greatest breadth	Greatest depth
Magdalenska gora			
Tumulus V, grave 29, Horse I	103*	48	39
Tumulus V, grave 29, Horse III	109	47	47
Tumulus V, grave 29, Horse III	109	47	47*
Szentes-Vekerzug			
Grave 6 or 8	101	48	45

* = approximately

Metatarsus	Greatest length	Breadth of the proximal end	Minimum breadth	Breadth of the distal end	Depth of the proximal end	Minimum depth	Depth of the distal end
Magdalenska gora							
Tumulus IV, grave 43	255*	45	27.5	—	41.5	23	—
Tumulus IV, grave 43	256	45	27.5	—	—	23	—
Tumulus V, grave 29, Horse I	260	—	—	47	43	24.5	36.5
Tumulus V, grave 29, Horse I	260*	—	27.5	—	44	24	—
Tumulus V, grave 29, Horse II	252.5	47	27	—	45.5	22.5	37
Tumulus V, grave 29, Horse II	252.5	47*	27	—	45*	22	37
Tumulus V, grave 29, Horse III	248	46	26.5	—	41	23.5	—
Szentes-Vekerzug							
Grave 6 or 8	254	46.5	27.5	47	45.5	22	—
Grave 6 or 8	254	—	28.5	47	—	22.5	34.5
Histria							
Number P. 18	275	51	30.5	51	49	26.1	37
Number P. 25	277.5	50	32	51.8	45.5	26	—
South-Russian finds:							
Neapol skifski							
	294	53	33.5	53	—	—	—
	284	53	31	52	—	—	—
	281	52	32	52	—	—	—
	274	52.5	37	52	—	—	—
	274	52	37.5	52	—	—	—
	270	—	33	51	—	—	—
	266	—	33	49	—	—	—
	262	47	30	47	—	—	—
	259	48.5	34	—	—	—	—
	259	50	31	49	—	—	—
	258	50	31	51	—	—	—
	257	48	36	—	—	—	—
	253	48	35	48	—	—	—
	251	—	35	—	—	—	—
	259	51	31	48	—	—	—
Gawrilowskoe gorodišče	256	51	31	49	—	—	—
	282	51	30	50	—	—	—
	254	44	29	46	—	—	—
	260	46	30	46	—	—	—
	252	46	30	46	—	—	—
Peresadowskoe gorodišče	269	49	30	50	—	—	—
Kamenskoe gorodišče	268	53	34	50	—	—	—
	260	52	32	51	—	—	—
	269	50	34	51.5	—	—	—
	255	45	30	48	—	—	—
	272	51	31	—	—	—	—
	251	46	31	49	—	23	—
	234	—	32	45	—	23	—
	247	46	34	—	—	—	—
	253	45	32	45	—	24	—
Olbia	274	51	33	—	—	—	—
	262	54	31	51	—	—	—
	273	49	32	50	—	—	—
	254	49	31	48	—	—	—
	252	48	32	47	—	—	—
	265	52	34	—	—	—	—
	273	52	32	50	—	—	—
	265	51	30	49	—	—	—
	268	—	31	47	—	—	—
	260	49	30	49	—	—	—
	261	48	29	47	—	—	—
	272	—	31	48	—	—	—
	259	—	30	47	—	—	—

	Greatest length	Breadth of the proximal end	Minimum breadth	Breadth of the distal end	Depth of the proximal end	Minimum depth	Depth of the distal end
Pantikapei	266	49	31	49	—	—	—
	258	50	31.5	50	—	—	—
	269	49	30	48	—	—	—
	258	50	31.5	50	—	—	—
	256	47	29	—	—	—	—
	266	51	32	49	—	—	—
	255	49	32.5	49	—	—	—
Ilupat	245	45	34	—	—	—	—
	258	46	32	47.5	—	—	—
	263	51	32	48	—	—	—
Mirmekii	251	—	31	48	—	—	—
	257	49	32	49	—	—	—
	265	48	31	48	—	—	—
	270	53	32.5	51	—	—	—
	265	49	30.5	48	—	—	—
	266	53	31	48	—	—	—
	271	50	31	49	—	—	—
	283	52	33	53	—	—	—
	283	51	32	50	—	—	—
	265	51	31	51	—	—	—
	263	—	33	53	—	—	—
Germonassa	256	46.5	29	—	—	—	—
Kery	254	47	29	47	—	—	—
Tanais	251	52	30	49	—	—	—
	267	—	32	50	—	—	—
	270	—	31.5	50	—	—	—
	256	—	32	48	—	—	—
	260	49.5	27.5	48	—	—	—
	271	50	32.5	—	—	—	—
	252	49	31	49	—	—	—
	255	51	31	51	—	—	—
	266	50	32.5	49	—	—	—
	259	46	32	48	—	—	—
	251	45	30.5	46	—	—	—
Geroewka	269	52	30.5	51	—	—	—
Kimmerik	252	49.5	30	48.5	—	—	—
Feodosia	265	48	29.5	48	—	—	—
Suiur-Tash	264	50	29	49	—	—	—
Fanagoria	262	47	30.5	47	—	—	—
Semidratnee gorodišče	267	50	30.5	50	—	—	—
	258	49.5	30	51	—	—	—
	264	49.5	30	49.5	—	—	—
Solokha (Northern Caucasus)	261	45	30	46	41*	24	34.5
	260*	48	29	45.6	—	22	34
Finds from kurgans of Altai Pazyryk	273	49	32	50	47	26.5	38
	261	50	30	50	50	27	39
	249	48.5	29.5	47.5	43.2	22.5	36
	264	51	32.5	51	48.5	27	35.5
	258	45.5	29	44.5	41.5	23.5	34.5
Other kurgans	279	56	34.5	55	53	29	40
	282.5	51	33	54	50.5	29	40
	271	46	30	48	45	25.5	35.5
	276	52	32	51	49	26	39
	284	53	33.5	54	50	28.5	41.5
	274	51	32.5	51.5	48	26.5	41
	272	52.5	34	53	50.5	27	39
	281	51	32	50.5	48	28	37.5
	266	48	30	50	47	·25	38

Os phalangis I ant.

	Sagittal length	Breadth of the proximal end	Minimum breadth	Breadth of the distal end	Depth of the proximal end	Minimum depth	Depth of the distal end
Magdalenska gora							
Tumulus V, grave 29, Horse II	76	47	32	42.5	34	17.5	24
Szentes-Vekerzug							
Grave 6 or 8	76	51	33.5	41	35.5	18	—

Os phalangis I post.

	Sagittal length	Breadth of the proximal end	Minimum breadth	Breadth of the distal end	Depth of the proximal end	Minimum depth	Depth of the distal end
Magdalenska gora							
Tumulus V, grave 29, Horse II	71	51	31	—	—	17	24.5
Szentes-Vekerzug							
Grave 6 or 8	74	52	30.5	39	37.5	17.5	—

Os phalangis II ant.

	Sagittal length	Breadth of the proximal end	Minimum breadth	Breadth of the distal end	Depth of the proximal end	Minimum depth	Depth of the distal end
Magdalenska gora							
Tumulus V, grave 29, Horse II	40	—	44	50.5	31	20.5	25.5
Szentes-Vekerzug							
Grave 6 or 8	38*	50	40.5	—	30	22	—

Os phalangis II post.

	Sagittal length	Minimum breadth	Breadth of the distal end	Depth of the proximal end	Minimum depth	Depth of the distal end
Magdalenska gora						
Tumulus V, grave 29, Horse II	40	44	50.5	31	20.5	25.5

Os phalangis III ant.

	Greatest length	Greatest breadth	Greatest depth
South-Russian finds:			
Neapol skifski	51	84	41
	59	87	44
	56	85	42
	56	84	40
	56	79	42
	49	80	37
	52	80	41.5
	56	87	41
	56	87	42
	53	78	39
	52	75	39
	51	81	38
Kamenskoe gorodišče	54	83	40
	55	75	40
	53	78	40
	51	77	37
	50	76	41
	48	79	36
	48	81	38
	53	78	39
	55	85	42
	53	81	36

	Greatest length	Greatest breadth	Greatest depth
Gawrilowskoe gorodišče	54	82	39
Peresadowskoe gorodišče	53	79	42
Olbia	53	81	38
	49	80	35
	52	80	40
	43	—	33
	54	80	38
	54	80	41
Pantikapei	49	79	38
	53	77	42
	50	82	38
	50	82	39
	50	80	37
	52	86	43
	50	73	38
	54	75	36
Lysa'a gora	51	82	39
Semidratnee gorodišče	53	83	43
	56	81	42
Tanais	60	98	46
	51	84	42
	52	80	39
	49	76	38

Os phalangis III post.

	Greatest length	Greatest breadth	Greatest depth
Magdalenska gora			
Tumulus V, grave 29, Horse II	64	—	33
Velemszentvid			
S. M. number: 54.499.1	—	69	36
South-Russian finds:			
Neapol skifski	60	79	43
	56	75	42
	58	74	42
	58	75	40
	54	68	40
	48	65	38
	53	75	37
	50	72	37
	52	72	38
	54	76	38
	57	76	40
	54	74	42
Kamenskoe gorodišče	56	78	39
	55	74	42
	55	75	42
	53	73	40
	56	75	42
	57	74	43
	54	80	38
	52	73	37
Peresadowskoe gorodišče	56	82	46
Olbia	56	75	40
	52	75	39
	50	77	38
	53	78	37
	57	—	41
	50	70	37
Pantikapei	51	71	36
	54	76	40
	54	74	39
	58	76	41
	53	71	39
	53	72	38
Mirmekii	58	85	42
	56	78	40
	61	81	45
	57	78	43
Feodosia	59	83	40.5
Semidratnee gorodišče	55	72	40
	53	72	39
	51	67	36

BIBLIOGRAPHY

AMSCHLER, J. W.
1932. Ausgrabungen von Polowzer-Pferden in Mittelasien. *Forschungen und Fortschritte*, vol. 8.
1934. Die ältesten Nachrichten und Zeugnisse über das Hauspferd in Europa und Asien. *Forschungen und Fortschritte*, vol. 10.
1949. Ur- und frühgeschichtliche Haustierfunde aus Österreich. *Archaeologica Austriaca*, Heft 3, pp. 3-100.

ANTONIUS, O.
1918. Die Abstammung des Hauspferdes und Hauesels. *Die Naturwissenschaften*, vol. 6.
1922. Grundzüge einer Stammesgeschichte der Haustiere. Jena.
1936. Zur Abstammung des Hauspferdes. *Zeitschrift für Tierzüchtung und Züchtungsbiologie*, vol. 34.

ARTSIKHOVSKII, A. V.
1947. Introduction in the archaeology. In Russian. Moscow.

BANNER, J.
1939. Data to the question of the horse's domestication. In Hungarian. Dolgozatok. Szeged. 15.

BELONOGOW, M. I.
1957. The morphological characteristics and the ways of improvement at the horse-breed of Akhal-Tekin. In Russian. Moscow.

BENDA, L.
1928. A velemszentividi östelep—Die urzeitliche Siedlung in Velemszentvid. Vasvármegyei Muzeum Természettudományi Osztályának évi jelentése. Szombathely.

BERNSTAM, A. N.
1948. Rock-carvings in Aravan and Ershi, the capital of Davan'. In Russian. *Sovjetskaja Etnografia*. Ferghana.

BIBIKOWA, W. I.
1958. The fauna of Olbia and its environs after the material of the excavations in 1935-48. In Ukrainian with Russian summary. *Archelogični pamatki URSR.* VII.
1962. The fauna of the settlement of Mikhailovka. In Ukrainian. IN: O. F. Lagodowska, O. G. Shaposhnikowa, M. L. Makarevich, *The settlement of Mikhailowka*. Kiew.

BÖKÖNYI, S.
1952. Les chevaux scythiques du cimetière de Szentes-Vekerzug. I. *Acta Archaeologica Hungarica*, vol. 2 pp. 173-83.
1954. Les chevaux scythiques du cimetière de Szentes-Vekerzug. II. *Acta Archaeologica Hungarica*, vol. 4, pp. 93-113.
1955. Les chevaux scythiques du cimetière de Szentes-Vekerzug. In Russian, French summary. *Acta Archaeologica Hungarica*, vol. 6, pp. 23-31.
1959. Die frühalluviale Wirbeltierfauna Ungarns (vom Neolithikum bis zur La-Tène-Zeit). *Acta Archaeologica Hungarica*, vol. 11, pp. 39-102.

BÖKÖNYI, S. AND KUBASIEWICZ, M.
1961. Neolithische Tiere Polens und Ungarns in Ausgrabungen. I. Das Hausrind. Budapest.

BOESSNECK, J.
1956. Tierknochen aus spätneolithischen Siedlungen Bayerns. *Studien an vor- und frühgeschichtlichen Tierresten Bayerns.* I. München.
1958a. Zur Entwicklung vor- und frühgeschichtlicher Haus- und Wildtiere Bayerns im Rahmen der gleichzeitigen Tierwelt Mitteleuropas. *Studien an vor- und frühgeschichtlichen Tierresten Bayerns.* II. München.
1958b. Herkunft und Frühgeschichte unserer mitteleuropäischen landwirtschaftlichen Nutztiere. *Züchtungskunde.* 30.

BOESSNECK, J. AND DAHME, E.
1959. Palaeopathologische Untersuchungen an vor- und frühgeschichtlichen Haustierfunden aus Bayern. *Tierärztliche Umschau*, vol. 14.

BOURDELLE, E.
1932. Notes ostéologiques et ostéometriques sur le cheval de Przewalski. *Bulletin de Muséum d'Histoire Naturelle*, vol. 2.

BRINKMANN, A.
1921. Equidenstudein I-II. Bergens Museums Aarbok 1919-20. Naturvidenskabelige Raekke, vol. 5.

CHUBB, S. H.
1913. The horse under domestication: its origin and the structure and growth of the teeth. American Museum of Natural History.

DARWIN, C.
1868. Animals and plants under domestication. London.

DEGERBÖL, M.
1935. Vore Pattedyr i Fortiden. *IN*. A. L. V. Manniche, Danmarks Pattedyr. Copenhagen.

DUERST, J. U.
1908. Animal remains from the excavations at Anau and the horse of Anau in its relation to the races of domestic horses. *IN*. R. Pumpelly, Explorations in Turkestan. 2. Washington, D. C.

EBHARDT, H.
1962. Ponies und Pferde im Röntgenbild nebst einigen stammesgeschichtlichen Bemerkungen dazu. *Säugetierkundliche Mitteilungen*, vol. 10.

EWART, J. C.
1905–06. The tarpan and its relationship with wild and domestic horses. *Proceedings of Royal Society of Edinburgh*, vol. 26.
1907. The derivation of the modern horse. *Quarterly Review London.* No. 411.
1909. The possible ancestors of the horse living under domestication. *Science*, vol. 30.

FALZ-FEIN, F. v.
1920. Das letzte Auftreten des Wildpferdes in Südrussland. *Sitzungsberichte der Gesellschaft Naturforschender Freunde zu Berlin 1919.*

FOLTINY, S.
1958. Velem-Szentvid, ein urzeitliches Kulturzentrum in Mitteleuropa. *Veröffentlichungen der Österreichischen Arbeitsgemeinschaft für Ur- und Frühgeschichte*, vol. 3.

FÖRSTER, U.
1960. Die Pferdephalangen aus dem keltischen Oppidum von Manching. *Studien an vor- und frühgeschichtlichen Tierresten Bayerns*. VIII. Munich.

FORSYTH-MAJOR, C. J.
1880. Beiträge zur Geschichte der fossilen Pferde. *Abhandlungen der Schweizerischen Paläontologischen Gesellschaft*, vol. 7.

FRAAS, E.
1902. Ausgrabungen eines römischen Brunnens bei Donnstetten O. A. Urach, nebst Untersuchungen über die dort gefundenen Hunde- und Pferderassen. *Fundberichte aus Schwaben*. 10.

FRANCK, I.
1875. Beiträge zur Rassenkunde unserer Pferde. *Landwirtschaftliche Jahrbücher.*

FRANK, K. G.
1962. Neue Funde des Pferdes aus dem keltischen Oppidum von Manching. *Studien an vor- und frühgeschichtlichen Tierresten Bayerns*. XIII. Munich.

GANDERT, O.-F.
1939. Das Pferd in der jüngeren Steinzeit Mittel- und Nordeuropas. *Compte Rendu IIeme Congrès Internationale des Sciences Anthropologiques et Ethnologiques Copenhague 1938*, pp. 226-27.

GAVILLET, E.
1945. Les animaux domestiques de l'époque romaine de Vidy-Lausanne. Lausanne.

GROMOVA, V. J.
1927. Material on the knowlege of the fauna of the Tripolje culture. In Russian. *Yezhegodnik Zoologicheskogo Muzeia Nauk SSSR.*
1949. The history of the horses (*Equus* genus) in early times. In Russian. *Trudy Paleontologicheskogo Instituta Akademia Nauk SSSR*, 17.
1959. On the skeleton of the tarpan (*Equus caballus* gmelini Ant.) and of other present day wild horses. I. In Russian with English summary. *Bulletin• Moskowskogo Obshchestwa Ispitatelei Prirody*, vol. 64.

HABERMEHL, K.-H.
1961. Die Altersbestimmung bei Haustieren, Pelztieren und beim jagdbaren Wild. Berlin-Hamburg.

HANČAR, F.
1956. Das Pferd in prähistorischer und früher historischer Zeit. *Wiener Beiträge zur Kulturgeschichte und Linguistik*, vol. 11.

HARTENSTEIN, E.
1956. Mit dem Pferd durch die Jahrtausende. Berlin.

HEPTNER, W.
1934. Notiz über den südrussischen Tarpan. *Zeitschrift für Säugetierkunde*, vol. 9.

HERMES, G.
1935. Das gezähmte Pferd im neolithischen und frühbronzezeitlichen Europa? I. *Anthropos*, vol. 30, pp. 803-823.
1936. Das gezähmte Pferd im neolithischen und frühbronzezeitlichen Europa? II. *Anthropos*, vol. 31, pp. 115-29.

HERRE, W.
1939. Beiträge zur Kenntnis der Wildpferde. *Zeitschrift für Tierzüchtung und Züchtungsbiologie*, vol. 44.

1956. Die Züchtungsbiologische Bedeutung neuer Erkenntnisse über Abstammung und Frühentwicklung von Haustieren. *Zuchtungskunde*, vol. 28.

1958. Die geschichtliche Entwicklung der Haustierzüchtung. *IN.* W. Zorn, *Tierzüchtungslehre*. Stuttgart.

1959. Der heutige Stand der Domestikationsforschung. *Naturwissenschaftliche Rundschau*.

1961. Grundsätzliches zur Systematik des Pferdes. *Zeitschrift für Tierzüchtung und Züchtungsbiologie*, vol. 75.

HESCHELER, K.

1930. Aus der Vorgeschichte der Säugetiere der Schweiz. *Jahrbuch der St.-Gallener Naturwissenschaftlichen Gesellschaft*, vol. 65.

1933. Die Fauna der neolithischen Pfahlbauten der Schweiz und des deutschen Bodenseegebietes nach neueren Forschungen. *Vierteljahresschrift der Naturforschenden Gesellschaft in Zürich*, vol. 78.

HESCHELER, K. AND KUHN, E.

1949. Die Tierwelt der prähistorischen Siedlungen der Schweiz. *IN.* O. Tschumi, ed., *Urgeschichte der Schweiz*, vol. I. Frauenfeld.

HILZHEIMER, M.

1912-13. Überblick über die Geschichte der Haustierforschung, besonders der der letzten 30 Jahre. *Zoologische Annalen*, vol. 5.

1920. Die Tierreste aus dem römischen Kastell Cannstatt bei Stuttgart und anderen römischen Niederlassungen in Württemberg. *Landwirtschaftliche Jahrbücher*, vol. 55.

1924. Die im Saalburgmuseum aufbewahrten Tierreste aus römischer Zeit. *Saalburgjahrbuch*, vol. 5.

1926. Natürliche Rassengeschichte der Haussäugetiere. Berlin.

1927. Unser Wissen von der Entwicklung der Haustierwelt Mitteleuropas. 16. *Bericht der Römisch-Germanischen Kommission*. 1925-1926.

1935. The evolution of domestic horse. *Antiquity*, vol. 9, pp. 133-39.

HOERNES, M.

1915. Krainische Hügelnekropolen der jüngeren Hallstattzeit. *Prähistorische Zeitschrift*, Jahrgang II, pp. 98-123.

HUPPERTZ, J.

1961. Untersuchungen über die Anfänge der Haustierzucht unter besonderer Berücksichtigung der Pferdezucht. *Anthropos*, vol. 56, pp. 14-30.

1962. Die frühe Pferdezucht in Ostasien. *Zeitschrift für Tierzüchtung und Züchtungsbiologie*, vol. 76.

IVANOV, S.

1954. Data about the horses of the Thracic tumulus-cemetery at Bresovo. In Bulgarian with French summary. *Godishnik na Muzeia v Plovdivski Okryg*. Plovdiv.

JOSIEN, T.

1955. La faune de la station de Saint-Romain. *Bulletin de la Societé Préhistorique Française*, vol. 52, pp. 177-86.

KELLER, C.

1913. Über Haustierfunde von La Tène. *Mitteilungden der Thurgauer Naturforschenden Gesellschaft*, vol. 20.

1923. La faune de la Tène. *IN.* P. Vouga, *La Tène—Monographie de la station*. Leipzig.

KIESEWALTER, L.

1888. Skelettmessungen an Pferden als Beitrag zur theoretischen Grundlage der Beurteilungslehre des Pferdes. Dissertation. Leipzig.

KRÄMER, H.

1900. Die Haustierfunde von Vindonissa. *Revue Suisse de Zoologie*, vol. 7.

KROMER, K.

1959. Brezje. Hallstättische Hügelgräber aus Brezje bei Trebelno. German text pp. 9-47. Ljubljana.

LA BAUME, W.

1953. Herkunft und älteste Kulturgeschichte der Haussägetiere. *IN.* W. Rothmaler, compiler, *Beiträge zur Frühgeschichte der Landwirtschaft*. I, pp. 53-67.

LEPIKSAAR, J.

1962. Die vor- und frühgeschichtlichen Haustiere Südschwedens. *Zeitschrift für Tierzüchtung und Züchtungsbiologie*, vol. 77.

LEUTHARD, F.

1930. Über eisenzeitliche Knochenreste (Küchenabfälle) von der Sissacherfluh (Baselland). *Ecologae Geologicae Helvetiae*, vol. 23.

LIEPE, H.-U.

1958. Die Pferde des Latène-Oppidums Manching. *Studien an vor- und frühgeschichtlichen Tierresten Bayerns*. IV. Munich.

LUNDHOLM, B.

1949. Abstammung und Domestikation des Hauspferdes. *Zoologiska Bidrag fran Uppsala*. XXVII.

LYDEKKER, R.
1912. The horse and its relatives. London.

MAGNAN, R.
1953. Épona, déesse gauloise des chevaux protectrice des cavaliers. Bordeaux.

MAREK, J.
1898. Das helvetisch-gallische Pferd und seine Beziehungen zu den prähistorischen und zu den rezenten Pferden. *Abhandlungen der Schweizerischen Paläontologischen Gesellschaft*, vol. 25.

MARKOV, G.
1958. Data to the history of the Mammals in Bulgaria. In Bulgarian with German summary. *Bulletin de l'Institut Zoologique de l'Academie des Sciences de Bulgarie*, vol. 7.

MATTHEW, W. D. AND CHUBB, S. H.
1913. Evolution of the Horse. Guide Leaflet Series. 36. American Museum of Natural History. New York.

MINNS, SIR E. H.
1913. Scythians and Greeks. Cambridge.

MISKE, K.
1896. The antiquities of Velem. In Hungarian. *Archaeologiai Értesitö.*
1907. The prehistoric settlement of Velem-szent-vid. In Hungarian. Vienna.
1908. Die prähistorische Ansiedlung Velem St. Vid. Vienna.

MOHR, E.
1959. Das Urwildpferd, *Equus przewalskii* Poljakoff 1881. *Die neue Brehm-Bücherei.* 249. Wittenberg.

MOREAU, J.
1958. Die Welt der Kelten. Stuttgart.

MOZSOLICS, A.
1953. Mors en bois de cerf sur le territoire du Bassin des Carpathes. *Acta Archaeologica Hungarica*, vol. 3, pp. 69-111.

MÜLLER, H.-H.
1955. Bestimmung der Höhe im Widerrist bei Pferden. *Jahresschrift für Mitteldeutsche Vorgeschichte*, no. 39, pp. 240-44.

NAUMANN, H. E.
1875. Die Fauna der Pfahlbauten im Starnberger See. *Archiv für Anthropologie*, vol. 8, pp. 1-48.

NEHRING, A.
1884. Fossile Pferde aus deutschen Diluvial-Ablagerungen und ihre Beziehungen zu den lebenden Pferden. Ein Beitrag zur Geschichte des Hauspferdes. *Landwirtschaftliche Jahrbücher*, vol. 13.

NOBIS, G.
1954. Zur Kenntnis der ur- und frühgeschichtlichen Rinder Nord- und Mitteldeutschlands. *Zeitschrift für Tierzüchtung und Züchtungs-biologie*, vol. 63.
1955. Beiträge zur Abstammung und Domestikation des Hauspferdes. *Zeitschrift für Tierzüchtung und Züchtungsbiologie*, vol. 64.
1962. Zur Frühgeschichte der Pferdezucht. *Zeitschrift für Tierzüchtung und Züchtungsbiologie*, vol. 76.

PÁRDUCZ, M.
1952. Le cimetière hallstattien de Szentes-Vekerzug. *Acta Archaeologica Hungarica*, vol. II, pp. 143-72.
1954. La cimetière hallstattien de Szentes-Vekerzug II. *Acta Archaeologica Hungarica*, vol. IV, pp. 25-91.
1955. La cimetière hallstattien de Szentes-Vekerzug III. *Acta Archaeologica Hungarica*, vol. VI, pp. 1-22.

PIÉTREMENT, C. A.
1870. Les origines du cheval domestique. Paris.

QUIBELL, J. E. AND OLVER, E.
1926. An ancient Egyptian horse. *Annales du Service des Antiquités de l'Egypte*, vol. 26.

REVILLIOD, P.
1926. Habitation gauloise de l'Oppidum de Genève: Les animaux domestiques. *Genava*, vol. 4.

RIEDEL, A.
1951. Risultati e significato degli studi di paleontologia degli animali domestici. *Natura, Rivista di Scienze Naturali di Milano*, vol. 42.

RUMJANCEV, B. T.
1936. Origin of domestic horse, *Bulletin de l'Academie des Sciences de l'URSS*, nos. 2-3.

RÜTIMEYER, L.
1863. Beiträge zur Kenntnis der fossilen Pferde und zur vergleichenden Odontographie der Huftiere überhaupt. *Verhandlungen der Naturforschenden Gesellschaft in Basel*, vol. 3.

SANSON, A.
1869. Nouvelles déterminations des espèces chevalines du genre *Equus*. *Comptes-rendus de l'Academie des Sciences,* vol. 69.

SCHARFF, R. F.
1909. On the Irish horse and its early history. *Proceedings of the Royal Irish Academy,* vol. 27.

SCHWARZ, E.
1922. Über europäische fossile Pferde und den Ursprung der Hauspferde. *Paläontologische Zeitschrift,* vol. 4.

SCHWERZ, F.
1918. Tierreste aus La Tène. *Anatomischer Anzeiger,* vol. 50.

SICKENBERG, O.
1962. Über die Grösse der pleistozänen Pferde der Caballus-Gruppe in Europa und Nordasien. *Eiszeitalter und Gegenwart,* vol. 12, pp. 99-124. English summary, p. 99.

SIMPSON, G. G.
1936. Horses and history. *Natural History,* vol. 38, pp. 276-88.
1951. Horses. New York.

SKORKOWSKI, E.
1938. Studies on the systematics of the horse. In Polish with German Summary. Kraków.
1946. Systematics of the horse and the principles of his breeding. In Polish with English summary. Krakow.
1956. Systematik und Abstammung des Pferdes. *Zeitschrift für Tierzüchtung und Züchtungsbiologie,* vol. 68.
1959. Erläuterungen zur Systematik des Pferdes. *Säugetierkundliche Mitteilungen,* vol. 10.
1962. Unterarten in den Pferdepopulationen und deren Frühgeschichte. *Zeitschrift für Tierzüchtung und Züchtungsbiologie,* vol. 76.
1958. Die ursprüngliche Rolle des Pferdes im Dienste des Menschen. *Akten des XVIII Internationalen Soziologenkongresses,* Nürnberg.

STEGMANN VON PRITZWALD, F. P.
1924. Die Rassengeschichte der Wirtschaftstiere. Jena.

STEJNEGER, L.
1904. Den celtiske pony, tarpanen og fjordhesten. *Naturen,* vol. 28.

STUDER, TH.
1900. Entwickelung der Hausthierzucht bei den Pfahlbauern. *Mittheilungen der Anthropologischen Gesellschaft in Wien,* vol. 30, pp. 106-08.

TASNÁDI KUBACSKA, A.
1960. Palaeopathology. In Hungarian. Budapest.

TRAININAS, D.
1933. Beiträge zur Kenntnis der Haustiere der römisch-keltischen Ansiedlung auf der Engehalbinsel bei Bern. Dissertation. Bern.

TSCHERSKI, J. D.
1892. Wissenschaftliche Resultate der von der kaiserlichen Akademie der Wissenschaften zur Erforschung des Janalandes und der Neusibirischen Inseln in den Jahren 1885 und 1886 ausgesandten Expedition. IV. *Memoires de l'Academie des Sciences St. Pétersbourg,* vol. 7, no. 40.

TSCHIRWINSKY, N.
1910. Die Entwicklung des Skeletts bei Schafen unter normalen Bedingungen, bei unzulänglicher Ernährung und nach Kastration der Schafböcke in frühem Alter. *Archiv für mikroskopische Anatomie und Entwicklungsgeschichte,* vol. 75.

VETULANI, T.
1939-40. Über den Farbenwechsel winterweisser Pferde. *Zeitschrift für Tierzüchtung und Züchtungsbiologie,* vol. 45.

VILLWOCK, W.
1962. Zur Frage der Anwendbarkeit statistischer Methoden für die Analyse frühgeschichtlicher Knochenfunde. *Zeitschrift für Tierzüchtung und Züchtungsbiologie,* vol. 77.

VITT, V. O.
1952. The horses of the kurgans of Pazyryk. In Russian. *Sovjetskaia Archeologia,* vol. 16.

VOGEL, R.
1933. Tierreste aus vor- und frühgeschichtlichen Siedlungen Schwabens. I. Tierreste aus den Pfahlbauten des Bodensees. *Zoologica,* vol. 82.

WAHLE, E.
1921. Die Besiedlung Südwestdeutschlands in vorrömischer Zeit nach ihren natürlichen Grundlagen. 12. *Bericht der Römisch-Germanischen Kommission.*

WILCKENS, M.
1888. Beitrag zur Kenntniss des Pferdegebisses. *Nova Acta Leopoldiana der Deutschen Akademie*, vol. 52.

YETTS, W. P.
1934. The horse: a factor in early Chinese history. *Eurasia Septemtrionalis Antiqua*, vol. 9, pp. 231-55.

ZADNEPROVSKI, YU. A.
1962. Rock-carvings about horses in Airimachtau. In Russian. Ferghana. *Sovjetskaja Etnografia*.

ZALKIN, V. I.
1952. To the investigation of the horses of the kurgans in the Altai. In Russian. *Materiali i issledovania po archeologii SSSR*, vol. 24.

1960a. Domestic and wild mammals of the northern adjacent area to the Black Sea in the early Iron Age. In Russian. *Materiali i issledovania po archeologii SSSR*, vol. 53.

1960b. Metapodial variation and its significance for the study of ancient horned cattle. In Russian with English summary. *Bulletin Moskovskogo Obshchestva Ispitatelei Prirody*, vol. 65.

1961. The variability of metapodialia in sheep. In Russian with English summary. *Bulletin Moskovskogo Obshchestva Ispitatelei Prirody*, vol. 66.

HUMAN SKELETAL REMAINS FROM SLOVENIA

J. Lawrence Angel

Smithsonian Institution, Washington, D.C.

HUMAN SKELETAL REMAINS FROM SLOVENIA

INTRODUCTION

THE NEW material described here includes nineteen male and ten female skulls and fragmentary skeletons of about 43 people from the site of Magdalenska gora, with a single male skeleton from nearby Bogenšperk (Wagensberg). Ten skeletons are linked with skulls of like sex; four divergences[1] in sex of skull and skeleton and many cases of supernumerary bones show that more than one skeleton could receive a single grave number. The opportunity for examining these remains came to me through the kindness of Dr. Hugh Hencken. And the work was carried out in the Peabody Museum of Harvard University with the permission and encouragement of Mr. Donald Scott, then director of the museum, and of the late Professor E. A. Hooton, chairman of the Department of Anthropology.[2]

As accompanying illustrations show, this is mainly an essay in restoration. Although facial fragments are present with most of the skulls,[3] their general preservation is so poor that only one cranium can be called complete: N/3683. The bone obviously suffered from leaching action of soil acids in burials affected by alternate winter soaking and summer sun-baking. This causes extensive warping as well as decay of spongy bone, and further small fragments may have been lost in excavation, packing, and transport. Warping was overcome through careful aligning of all points in sagittal and transverse planes after the vault and base had been assembled; through breaking up all large warped segments into smaller pieces; and through use of Alvar synthetic resin for impregnation and glueing: Alvar hardens slowly enough and is cohesive and adhesive enough to allow a molding process of the assembled warped skull.[4] When warping involves only plain pressure flattening, correction is successful. This is clear in skull N/3721 and connects with a tendency for dolichocrane skulls to be crushed laterally and marked brachycranes anteroposteriorly and superiorly under earth pressure. But most warping includes twisting impossible to correct completely, as in N/3703.

Furthermore, in order to wring any coherent information from this most interesting material it was necessary to fill in the most critical lacunae with plasticine, according to detail found on other similar crania and the surrounding bone contours. *Hence all measurements are tentative.*[5] Errors introduced by earth-distortion, its correction, and by restoration in individual skulls should cancel out in the mean measurements of the males, though errors would increase variability.

[1] N/3719, N/3706, N/3796, and N/3709.

[2] In addition to the preceding I should like to thank Dr. Alice Brues, Dr. H. L. Shapiro, Dr. J. H. Gaul, Dr. Božo Škerlj, and Dr. J. B. Birdsell for divers suggestions, help, and criticisms which I may not always have followed. For much-valued help in preparation of skeletal material and for recording and ordering of data I thank my wife.

[3] Of 29 skulls 48.3% are crania, 27.6% calvariae with facial fragments, 13.8% calvariae, 10.3% calvae. 65.5% are in poor condition, 31.0% in fair condition, and only one skull in good condition. This is the normal state for earth burials in temperate and Mediterranean climates.

[4] For a summary of this technique see Angel, 1949. Besides proper cleaning, minute anatomical identification, and ordered assembling, the key to skull preservation is negative pressure impregnation of friable bone with hardening plastic. This hardening process was outlined to me in Athens by Dr. E. Breitinger, and is presumably a product of the Munich anthropology Laboratory under Mollison. The Shawinigan Products Corporation no longer makes Alvar 7/70 soluble in acetone. But one can use Formvars 15/95 or 12/85 soluble in toluene—95% ethanol (60:40 by weight) or in glacial acetic acid (too strong for bone) or in chloroform or in ethylene chloride—solvents hard to get in a remote mountain town and more toxic than acetone. We are still looking for a true substitute for Alvar 7/70.

[5] The technique of measuring is that in use at Peabody Museum under Dr. E. A. Hooton, and follows definitions in Martin, 1928, vol. II. But auricular height is measured from Frankfurt plane to vertex. And for facial angles the point where a straightedge touching the lateral walls of the pyriform aperture crosses the upper edge of the nasal spine is substituted for Martin's bone-buried nasospinale. Orbital breadth is measured to dakryon, to be remembered in comparison with the German and Slavic authors quoted in this paper.

Other cranial material from Slovenia includes six skulls measured by von Luschan from the site of Laibach Moor, more accurately the pile-dwelling settlement at Ig south of Ljubljana,[6] possibly of Late Bronze Age date contemporary with Terremare, or later. U. C. Vram (1903) has published five skulls of late Hallstatt date from Vače(Watsch), nineteen skulls of Roman and probably Roman date from Slepsech, Dernove, and Ljubljana, ten of early Slavic and possibly Slavic date from Veldes, Heiligenberg, and Gorianchi, twenty-two 14th to 16th century Mediaeval skulls and twenty-one non-ancient probably Mediaeval skulls from Ljubljana. A. Weisbach's (1912) 19th century "modern" Slovenes seriated by Morant (1928) must be considered descendants of Vram's last two groups.

Comparative material from outside Slovenia includes the Bavarian Mesolithic decapitate skulls from Ofnet, Kaufertsberg, and Hohlenstein described by Scheidt (1923) and Gieseler (1938), an East Balkan–Ukrainian Chalcolithic series from data of Drončilov (1924), Doniči, Jaranov (1939), Pittard (1903), and Popov, Austrian Hallstatt and Bohemian La Tène series compiled by Coon (1939, Tables 32, 33) from various German authors and from B. Hellič, parallel data from Toldt (1912) and Petri (1935), South Illyrians of Hallstatt through Roman date from the Glasinac plateau in S. E. Bosnia described by Weisbach (1897, 1907), and Schwidetsky (1940), Classical Greeks from Corinth, Attica, Boeotia, and Macedonia (Angel, 1960) and H. L. Shapiro's 17th–19th century Carinthians (1929) from Greifenberg in the Drave valley, and their Medieval ancestors from Ptuj (Ivaniček, 1951).

DESCRIPTION

The small number of Illyrian skulls from Magdalenska gora make it wise to describe each one singly before comparing the average inhabitant of that area with averages for other periods in Slovenia and those for groups outside Slovenia shown in Tables III and IV respectively. Tables I and II contain the individual and average measurements of the Magdalenska gora skulls and the mean measurements of the skeletons. In analyzing the crania the six morphological types arbitrarily worked out in detail for ancient Greeks (Angel, 1944, 1960) give a useful descriptive standard, in spite of peculiarities of West Balkan populations which such crudely inclusive types cannot adequately express. Type percentages for various series are listed in Table V.

Type A, called Basic White, is a modernization of the more linear upper palaeolithic variety. It includes rugged dolichocranes like Coon's Megalithic or Deniker's Atlanto–Mediterranean and other more typically East

[6] F. von Luschan, 1881. But see also U. C. Vram, 1903, and N. Zupanič, 1919, the latter for his perpetuation of von Luschan's rejected speculation that these were negroid skulls. Vram's skulls #1, 2, and 3 are obviously I, III, and IV of von Luschan's work, and his mention of iron combines with von Luschan's account of many chipped stone tools with little bronze (though including a short sword and decorated knife) to blur dating.

Mediterranean low-headed, low-faced, and broad-jowled dolichocranes. The skull is large, coarse, rugged, and long, low, pentagonoid, ill-filled, flat-sided, gabled, and flattened in the region of lambda. A low and sloping forehead marked by heavy and angular browridges surmounts the strong-jowled face. This has rectangular orbits, robust cheekbones, a short, coarse, almost chaemerrhine nose with straight profile and deep nasion depression, a U-shaped palate, strong-chinned jaw, and well-developed teeth. Greek Basic Whites are close to Chalcolithic Palestinians from Megiddo, Siculans, and Sardinians, somewhat resemble British Neolithic series and more distantly resemble Early Dynastic Mesopotamians and Neolithic Swedes; this element is basic in the Near East from Natufian and Jericho levels on. This type's importance in the present study is its dominance in the Early Iron Age graves of Cephallenia at the mouth of the Adriatic (Angel, 1943), its occurrence at Novilara on the central Adriatic coast of Italy and its share in the Mesolithic Mediterranean populations of Israel, Syria, Jordan and Europe (Coon, 1939, after McCown and Vallois).

Type B, the paedomorphic Classic Mediterranean of Sergi, has a small, gracile, and just dolichocrane skull, pentagonoid, large-bossed,

with relatively low, vertical, and narrow forehead, prominent occiput, and weak muscle markings. The face is narrow, leptoprosopic, and tapering, with square orbits delicately enclosed by compressed cheekbones, small and narrow nose with little nasion depression, pinched and incipiently prognathous mouth region, lightly worn teeth linked with an overbite, and weak and compressed lower jaw with shallow and pointed chin. The gracile Mediterranean is practically identical with ancient Libyans and modern Sicilians, and close to Dynastic Upper Egyptian groups. Its importance here is not only its fairly close association with Basic Whites in Sicily, Iron Age Italy, and the Ionian Islands, but also in the Bavarian Mesolithic series and in the Eastern Balkans and Black Sea coasts where Coon (1939, p. 617) identifies a Pontic Mediterranean type important in the Neolithic-Chalcolithic series from North Bulgaria and Bessarabia shown in Table IV.

Type D is called Nordic-Iranian since it resembles skulls of Iron Age Nordic and Corded types and others approximating Late Bronze Age Iranians and Coon's Cappadocian type (Coon, 1939, pp. 137, 176). The well-filled ovoid-ellipsoid braincase is long-headed, high, long-based, and muscular, with capacious but receding forehead and peculiarly deep occiput. The rectangular outline of the large and leptoprosopic face goes with slightly drooping orbits and retreating cheekbones dominated in profile by a big, hawklike nose. A long, tilted, and high-arched palate combines with orthognathous mouth profile, and the strong jaw is marked by its cleft chin and strong angles. Nordic-Iranians show virtual identity with Bavarian Reihengräber skulls, and close resemblances to Anglo-Saxons, Irish monks, and Northern Iranians. The type's diagnostic value for the Magdalenska gora material concerns possible overland connections between Illyrians and Greeks much less than identification in Slovenia of "Hallstatt Nordic" traits whose eventual origin is in South Russia or further east and south in Iran. Such traits will of course be transmitted separately in individuals: the type is a concept only.

Type F is called Dinaric-Mediterranean because although it is "dinaricised" in Coon's sense (1939, 1950) it seldom has a completely Alpine braincase and is *not* deformed. The byrsoid and high mesocrane skull vault is short, high, narrow-based, with constricted forehead and non-projecting and high-placed occipital bone, and shallow glenoid fossa. The face is big and high with elongated hexagonal outline, marked by big, slightly drooping orbits and slightly flaring cheekbones. A long and thin nose whose profile continues that of the forehead, a high palate with crowded teeth, and the long and deep jaw all emphasize height of face. The type stands between dinaricised Mediterranean series of Lower Egypt and of Early Neolithic coastal Macedonia and Anatolian, Cypriote, and Balkan dinaricised Alpine groups. It is relevant in any discussion of inhabitants of Slovenia since this general region has often been considered the home of European Dinarics.

Type E, called Mixed Alpine, combines generalized Mediterranean with Alpine traits in an opposite fashion to Dinaric-Mediterraneans. The mesocrane braincase is notably large and well-filled, long-based as well as broad, with a peculiarly long, broad, and inflated frontal bone, an extensive obelion-lambda plane region, and well-filled temporal areas. The massive forehead dominates the low and strongly orthognathous face. Broad but slightly sloping orbits are bounded by weak cheekbones and abut on a low-bridged mesorrhine nose with high root. The large but shallow jaw gives paedomorphic impression, increased by a tendency toward an overbite. Mixed Alpines are closely similar to Romano-Etruscans, and besides approximations to Scythians, Merovingian Franks, and Basques, come closer to the *average* individual of Magdalenska gora than do any other of these types.

Type C, the Alpine, includes both paedomorphic and massive European Alpines and both high-headed and low-vaulted Near Eastern Alpines. The medium-sized short-headed vault is shortened in all segments, not high, and spheroid, short ovoid, or sphenoid in *norma verticalis*. The forehead is broad, the occiput is somewhat flat and marked by a strong torus, and the sidewalls bulge. The low and orthognathous face has a rounded square outline, and is characterized by relative "flatness" with laterally strong cheekbones and a notably non-salient nose generally with low root and bridge and concave profile. Marked orthognathy goes with short and low palate, a square jaw with strong chin, and an edge-to-edge bite accompanied by worn teeth. Alpines are much closer to "recent" Carinthians than to Greeks as a whole and resemble adequately the mediaeval Hythe series, foothill Bavarians, and Early Neolithic and Bronze Age eastern Cypriotes. This type's importance in this study is self-evident: it is in the heart of the modern Alpine area.

Table V's comparison of the percentages of these six types among 105 Greeks of Classic date with those among 30 individuals from Magdalenska gora stresses the vastly stronger Alpine and weaker Mediterranean elements in the Illyrian group. But this comparison also suggests existence of an important Nordic-Iranian minority in both groups linked with corresponding lack of any *developed* Dinaric type in either group at this period. Individual descriptions follow.

Type A: Basic White. Of the three rugged Mediterranean skulls N/3686 is the only male (Tumulus IV, grave 10). This is a middle-aged and fairly large ellipsoid dolichocrane with constricted forehead and a low, incipiently prognathous, and narrow-nosed face marked by strong cheekbones, oblong orbits, straight and high-bridged nose with small and grooved nasal spine, and a fairly broad jaw. The chin is shallow and of medium prominence, six teeth were lost in life, and those remaining show medium wear (marked on the incisors), one caries, one abscess, a slight tendency toward shovel incisors, and an edge bite (illustrated). Except for too well-filled vault and leptorrhine nose N/3686 conforms exactly to Basic White criteria, but is less crude and exaggerated than is Ig skull I or Ofnet skull (4) K 1818 which it resembles (von Luschan, 1881; Scheidt, 1923).

N/3702 (Tumulus X, grave 3) is a young adult female skull vault, ellipsoid, high, angular in profile and with a fragmentary jaw suggesting low rather than high face. She resembles the preceding male, N/3686.

N/3726 (Tumulus V, grave 24) is a long ellipsoid calvaria of a young adult female noteworthy for its height, flat sides, lambdoid flattening, and scaphoid sagittal region, thus

tending in a "Megalithic" direction. It is not dissimilar to Ofnet K 1821.

Type B: gracile Mediterranean. N/3699 (Tumulus IV, grave 58) is an ovoid young adult calvaria, low mesocrane, of intermediate morphology, with pointed mastoid processes and a light jaw with marked teeth wear, loss of molars and an indicated edge bite (illustrated).

N/3716 (Tumulus X, grave 32) is a pentagonoid middle-aged male calvaria, with long mastoids, marked occipital curve, narrowed skull base, narrow and slightly pinched forehead, and long and narrow jaw suggesting a pinched face. Teeth show marked wear, with four molars lost in life (illustrated). As a whole N/3716 shows Dinaric-Mediterranean trends as seen in some of the North Bulgarian Gumelnitsa period crania and in the Macedonian Neolithic cranium from Servia (Angel, 1942).

N/3713, (Tumulus X, grave 26) a young adult female cranium, has a rounded pentagonoid mesocrane valut with full forehead and protrusive skull base, and a narrow face with rounded square orbits, tilted and hyperbolic palate, slight alveolar prognathism, atypically deep and long jaw, medium overbite, and good teeth showing slight wear (illustrated). This skull shows fairly close similarity to Ofnet K 1811 and faintly recapitulates N/3716's Dinaric-Mediterranean tendencies.

Type D: Nordic-Iranian. N/3711, (Tumulus X, grave 20) a middle-aged male cranium with much restored face, illustrates the Balkan-Greek version of the more easterly Iranian type, having a much better filled vault than the latter. This skull's salient features include a large ellipsoid (-byrsoid) vault with almost cylindrical coronal section and "full" lower occiput. The beaked nose is set in a high, long-jawed, and probably narrow-jowled face with good teeth showing medium wear (illustrated).

N/3712 (Tumulus X, grave 25) is the pentagonoid (-ovoid) calvaria of a young adult male of medium-tall stature. The skull shows a full occiput, a cylindrical tendency like N/3711, a rectangular face with parabolic palate, clearcut chin, medium overbite, and excellent teeth with slight wear. A healed wound depression pits deeply just above the left fronto-malar suture and a crescentic slash through the mid-frontal zone was made

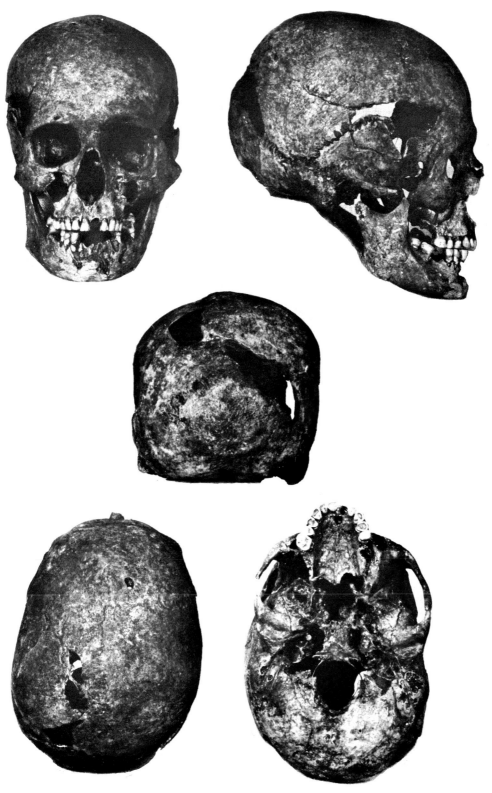

Fig. 1. N/3686 is a male skull showing Basic White (A 3) traits comparable with the linear element in latest Palaeolithic populations.

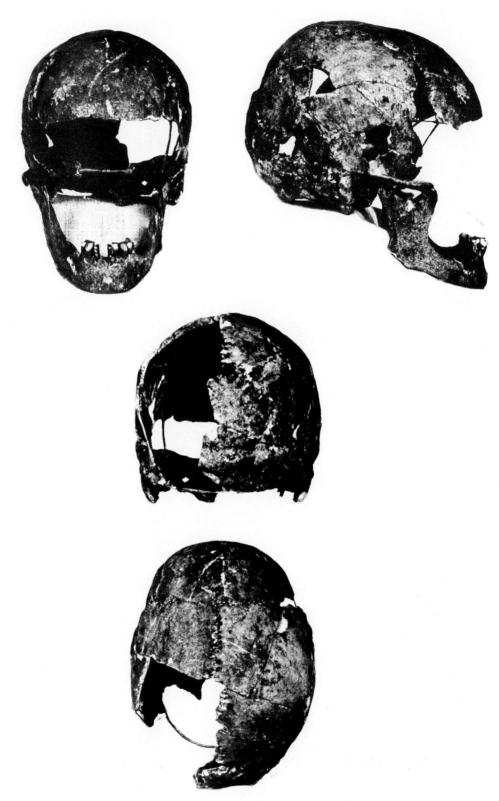

FIG. 2. N/3699 is a male showing gracile Mediterranean (B 1) linearity.

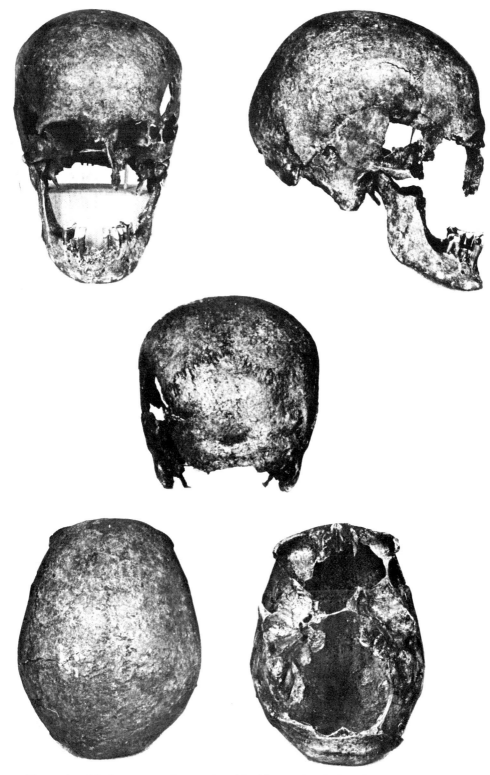

FIG. 3. N/3716 is a Mediterranean (B 2) male with rising vault, pinched forehead, and long jaws as in the Dinaric-Mediterranean (F1) trend in earliest Neolithic Macedonians or East Balkan groups.

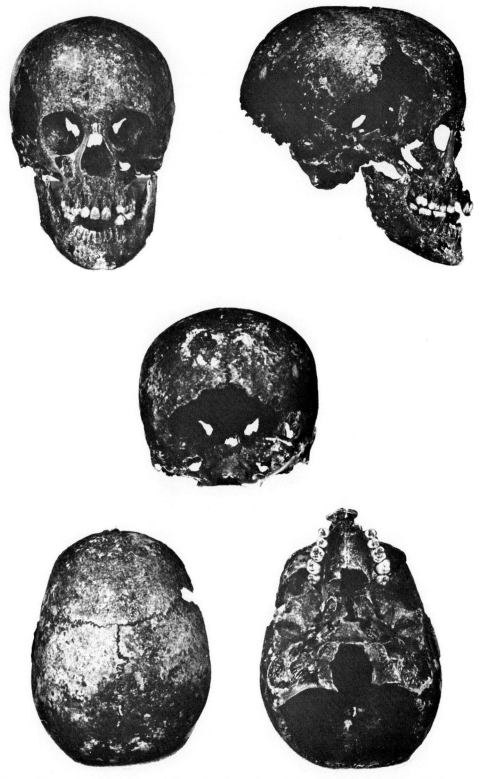

FIG. 4. N/3713 is a Mediterranean (B 2) female version of the preceding skull, but with lower and fuller vault.

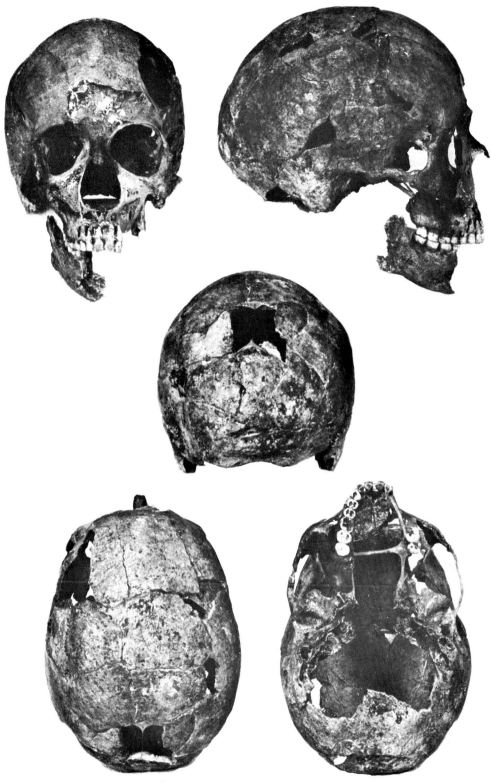

Fig. 5. N/3711 is a male showing Iranian traits (D 3) in a Balkan or Danubian version of Mediterranean. Note resemblances to N/3719.

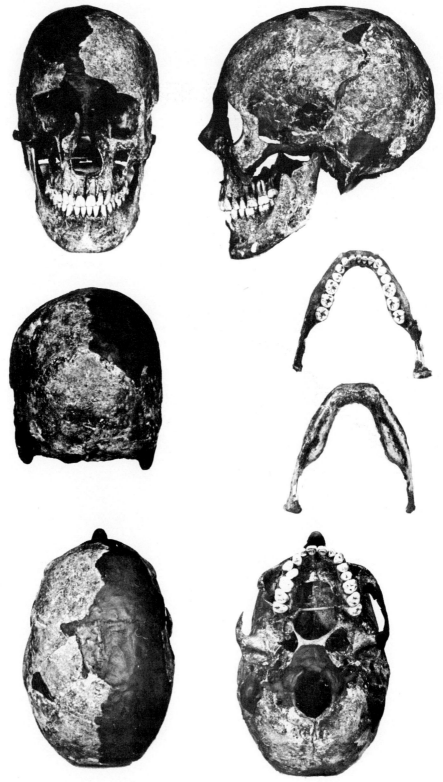

Fig. 6. N/3714, a Hallstatt Nordic (D 5) male with huge teeth, carries Iranian and Corded and some latest Palaeolithic traits.

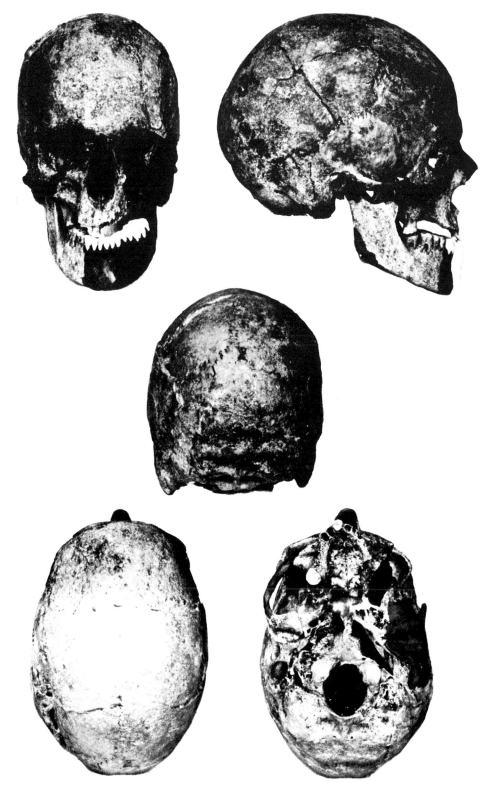

FIG. 7. N/3721, Corded Nordic (D 2) male with poor teeth, resembles both the preceding (N/3714 and 3711) emphasizing similarities with Kurgan skulls from Kazakhstan to the Danube. All three are from Tumulus X.

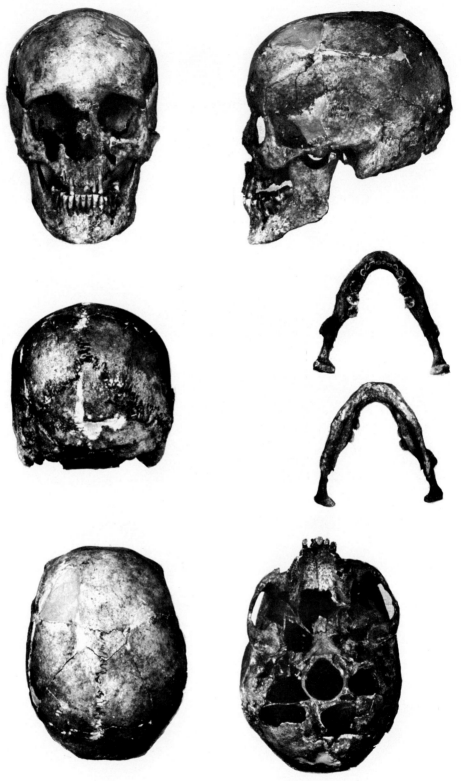

Fig. 8. N/3678 is a female skull facially comparable with the preceding (D 1) but with fuller vault having Mixed Alpine traits (E 1).

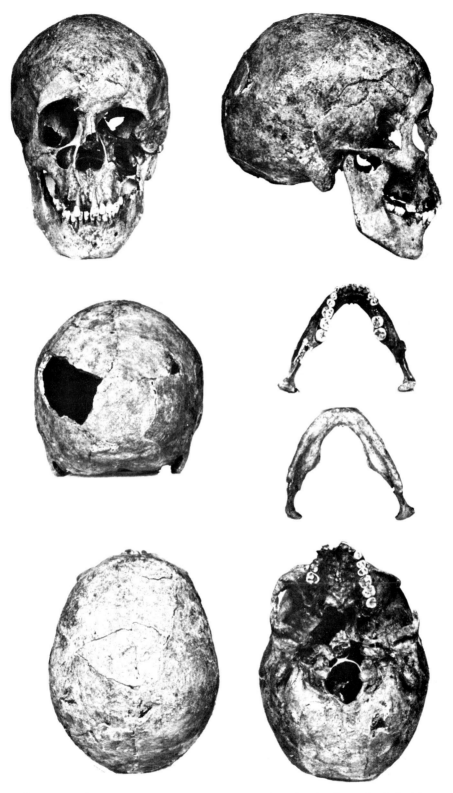

Fig. 9. N/3719, a big Dinaric-Mediterranean (F 3) male with family trait similarities to N/3711, has parallels with early Macedonians.

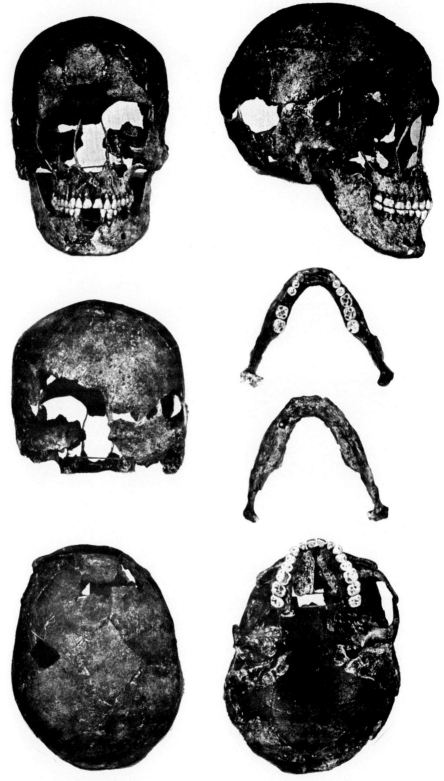

FIG. 10. N/3703 is a massive male of Mixed Alpine (E 2) form with Palaeolithic size traits including large teeth like N/3714.

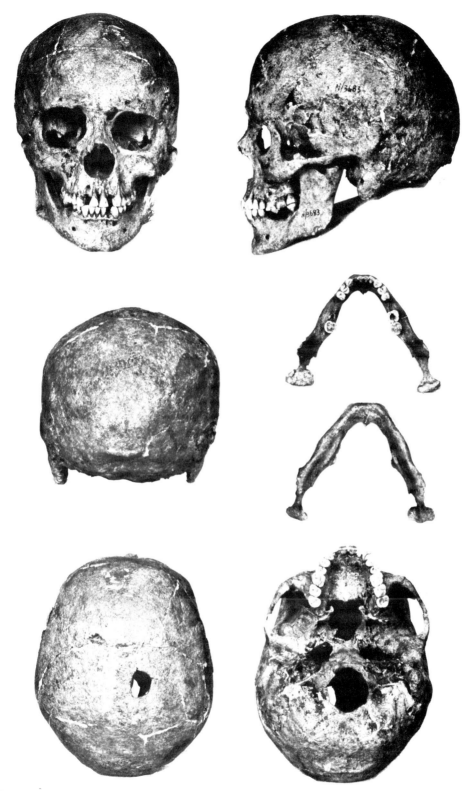

FIG. 11. N/3683 is a broad-skulled male typifying a Central European Alpine (C 1) norm with latest Palaeolithic background as at Solutré and Ofnet. Trephination and temporomandibular joint destruction may each link with mastoid and middle ear infection.

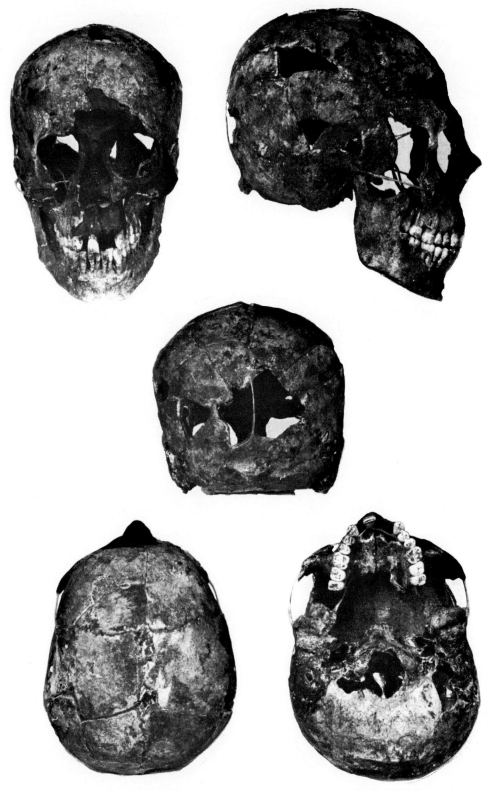

Fig. 12. N/3691 is a big-faced Alpine (C 3) male with chiefly Mesolithic parallels.

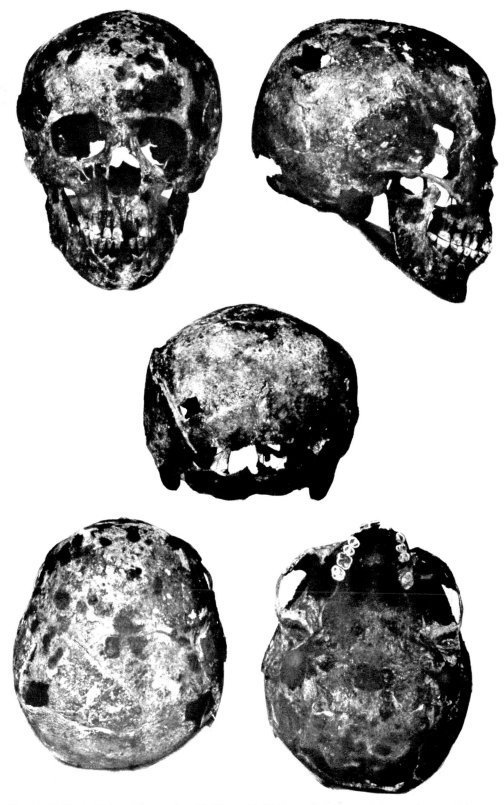

FIG. 13. N/3704, Alpine (C 1) male with Dinaroid (F 2) vault height and face traits, parallels one of the Eastern Alpine (C 4) tendencies in Neolithic Cyprus and the later Eastern Mediterranean.

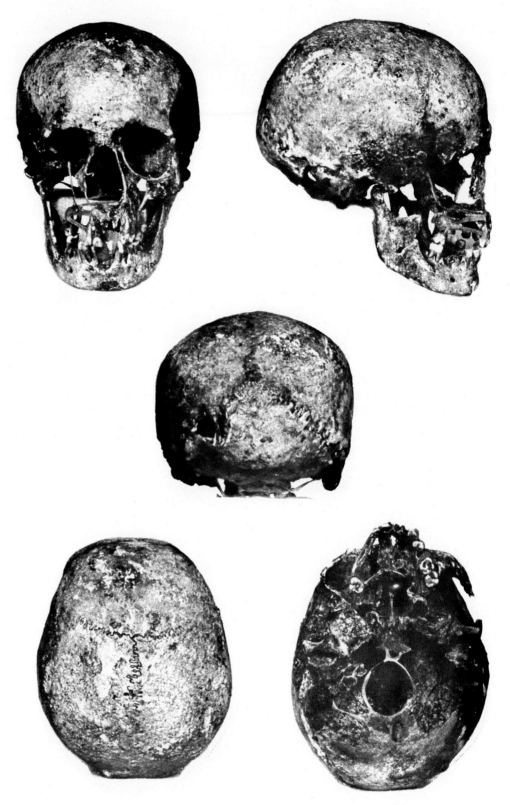

FIG. 14. N/3722 is a male of European Alpine form (C 1).

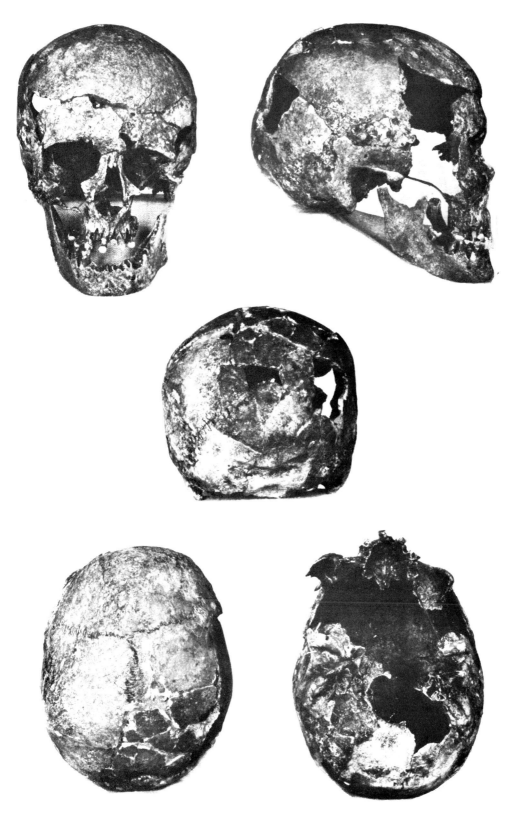

FIG. 15. N/3709 is a female (C 1) quite similar to the preceding skull in general trend.

FIG. 16. On the left side are the unhealed trephination and left mastoid opening of N/3683. The top center shows the old healed wound over the left orbit and the new sword-slash (?) across the forehead of N/3712. The top right shows a slight degree of tibial retroversion, normal today too; the bottom center shows vertebral osteophytes in the *ligamenta flava*; and the bottom right shows bone response to intervertebral disk herniation; these three are all from N/8548 in Tumulus X graves 32–33 at Magdalenska gora.

through green bone, possibly at time of death (illustrated, last plate). The skeleton shows average stature (170.5) and robusticity and eurycnemia.

N/3714 (Tumulus X, grave 28), the large cranium of a young adult male, is noteworthy for its great length and height, its ovoid vault with retreating forehead and deep occiput, and flat sides with rounded vertex. The high, deep-jawed, strongly orthognathous, and rectangular face has high square and scarcely tilted orbits and a big nose which was certainly narrow-bridged and very high. The broad and very high tilted palate and massive jaw are scarcely large enough for huge teeth of good quality with very few caries and slight wear, some crowding, and a slight overbite. Except for these teeth N/3714 (illustrated) exemplifies ideally the Hallstatt Nordic type. The accompanying skeleton is unusually tall (180 cm.) with massive long bones, platymeria, eurycnemia, and bowed radius and ulna.

N/3721 (Tumulus X, grave 57), a middle-aged male cranium, has an exceedingly high and flat-sided ellipsoid vault with high rounded forehead, deep rounded occiput and rounded vertex. The narrow, relatively small, and strongly orthognathous face is marked by low, elliptical, and drooping orbits with retreating cheekbones, very prominent thin nose, deep narrow and tilted jaw, and incipiently edentulous palate whose remaining teeth with those of the jaw are of good quality, with marked wear and an edge bite. This skull (illustrated) shows clearly the existence of "Corded" traits in a Hallstatt Nordic amalgam.

N/3678 (Destroyed graves FF) is the cranium of a middle-aged adult female, mesocrane, ellipsoid (-ovoid), with broad forehead and skull base and rounded scaphoid vertex. The tapering rectangular face has square tilted orbits, small cheekbones, large nose, slight alveolar prognathism, strong-jowled jaw, edge bite, and markedly worn teeth with five lost in life and five carious (illustrated).

Type F: Dinaric-Mediterranean. N/3719 (Tumulus X, grave 37) is the only clear example of this type, and is a large middle-aged male cranium. The ovoid (-byrsoid) vault is notable for its size, for its low and pinched forehead, for deeply down-bulging occiput, long mastoids, and almost cylindrical coronal section. The face is more rectangular than the expected hexagonal outline, with high rhomboid orbits, large concavo-convex nose noteworthy less for prominence than for extensive subnasal gutters, and prognathous mouth region emphasized by the heavy jaw's tilt and retreating chin with medium overbite. The teeth show medium wear with one lost, two caries and two abscesses of which one above the fused root of the upper third molar penetrated the floor of the maxillary sinus. A round wound depression pits the left frontal region, and a peculiar erosion of the outer table in the region of lambda (more carious than osteoporotic) might possibly indicate an infection deep to the galea aponeurotica. On the whole N/3719 (illustrated) is transitional from the Nordic-Iranian group, showing definite, "family" similarities with N/3711, and is by no means a modern Dinaric.

Type E: Mixed Alpine. N/3685 (Tumulus IV, grave 3) is the mesocrane ellipsoid calvaria of a young adult male, noteworthy for its capacious roundness, steep forehead, sagittal ridge, and delicate jaw suggesting a low face. The skeleton is tall (174 cm.) orthorachic in the lumbar region, and shows a definite femoral pilaster.

N/3692 (Tumulus IV, grave 30) is a very fragmentary cranium of an old adult male, long and massive, with capacious and expansive frontal bone. The orthognathous face appears to have been broad and is fairly large, with square orbits flanked by large but retreating cheekbones, big nose with massive root, and relatively small lower face with medium-worn good teeth, high parabolic palate and edge bite.

N/3697 (Tumulus IV, grave 55b), a young adult male cranium lacking frontal and upper face, has a broad vault with rounded vertex and occiput, and a well-cut jaw and maxilla, with sharp triangular chin, strong jowls, an edge bite, and good teeth with medium wear and two lost in life.

N/3703 (Tumulus X, grave 6) is the slightly twisted cranium of the middle-aged male, noteworthy for large size, ovoid (-pentagonoid) outline, low forehead, broad base, almost flat sidewalls, and incipiently roof-shaped vertex. The broad hexagonal face has a heavy lower segment with large palate containing excellent teeth showing medium wear, one lost, one carious, and an edge bite (illustrated). Like N/3692, N/3703 shows both Upper Palaeolithic strength and length with Alpine fullness and massiveness, and partly for this reason shows distant resemblance to Ofnet K 1800.

N/3706 (Tumulus X, grave 12), a middle-aged male calvaria with light jaw fragment, closely approaches N/3685, but with lambdoid-obelion flattening and incipiently projecting occiput to break the rounded contour.

N/3681 (Destroyed graves, LL), a fragmentary young adult female calvaria, is a blunt pentagonoid mesocrane with wide forehead, complete metopic suture, and jaw with slightly flaring angles and medium teeth wear.

N/3696 (Tumulus IV, grave 54), is a sub-adult female calvaria, ovoid, mesocrane, well-rounded, with sharply curved occiput and slight teeth wear.

N/3697 (Tumulus IV, grave 55a), another young adult female calvaria, ovoid and brachycrane, is marked by relatively large jaw and teeth showing medium wear. All the female Mixed Alpines have Mediterranean traits more superficially obvious than are Alpine ones.

Type C: Alpine. N/3683, (Destroyed graves, HH), the best preserved cranium of the series, is a late middle-aged male. The broad vault is blunt pentagonoid in form, with expansive forehead, arched vertex, slight obelion-lambda flattening, well-curved occiput with sharp inion, and long mastoids. The broad face is more square than hexagonal, with oblong orbits, retreating cheekbones, thick, straight-profiled nose, slightly prognathous mouth and strong jaw with bilateral and non-projecting chin and flaring angles. Good teeth show medium wear, two caries, three abscesses, and four teeth lost in life. Pathology of the left temporo-mandibular joint includes erosion of the articular eminence and flattening and lipped plaque formation on both eminence and condyle with shortening of the neck of the condyle. The left mastoid process shows an oval perforation on its antero-lateral surface, there is considerable enlargement of the left mastoid emissary foramen, and at apex just to the right of the sagittal suture an oval trephination through the thinned and slightly pitted parietal shows neatly cut, unhealed edges without bevel.[7] N/3683 (illustrated) is closely comparable to Ofnet K 1809 and resembles K 1800 slightly.

N/3691 (Tumulus IV, grave 25), a middle-aged adult male, has black carbonized patches most obvious on the front of the vault with gritty ashlike material adhering to some of them. This is a large and notably low and wide sphenoid (-ovoid) brachycrane, with low wide forehead and full temporals and cerebellar bulge of the non-flattened occiput. The face approaches hexagonal, with oblong orbits ringed by laterally flaring cheekbones, a thick-rooted concave nose, incipient total facial prognathism accented by medium alveolar prognathism of the strongly tilted mandible and by a retreating chin, and an excellent dentition with medium (-pronounced) teeth wear and an edge bite (illustrated). The skeleton shows short stature, (165 cm.) with very rugged musculature, eurymeria, mesocnemia, and squatting facets. The skull is similar to Ofnet K 1806.

N/3704 (Tumulus X, grave 7) a young adult male cranium, is a relatively small sphenoid brachycrane, high, with a short, flatly curved, down-bulging occiput marked by a large hook-line inion. The much-broken face is rounded square in outline, relatively low, with square and level orbits, non-protrusive cheekbones, long nose broad at root and bridge, and slight midfacial protrusion with medium alveolar prognathism of the jaw and retreating chin. Teeth show medium wear, three caries, medium crowding, and an edge bite. Although N/3704 (illustrated) shows in its occiput, orbital height, and perhaps in lower facial convexity traits which are apparently Dinaric, the skull is too chaemeprosopic and thick-nosed to be so classified. The skeleton shows medium-tall stature (174 cm.).

N/3722 (Tumulus X, grave 64), is a young adult male cranium, heavy, medium-sized, low, of blunt ovoid form, relatively narrow-based, with low and wide forehead and slight lamb-

[7] Possibly this was a final and fatal attempt to relieve symptoms of a chronic infection which might have started in the middle ear. The effects are much less severe than those seen in the chronic otitis media of an almost contemporary Late Bronze Age Irishman from Knockast, described by H.O'N. Hencken and H. L. Movius, 1934, p. 268.

doid flattening. The fragmentary face is hexagonal, with rhomboid orbits, low and wide nose root, slight midfacial prognathism, and light and narrow jaw with slight overbite. The teeth show slight wear and five caries (illustrated). The skeleton is notably tall (181 cm.), with heavy long bones, eurycnemia, and squatting facets.

N/3725 (Tumulus IV, grave II, isolated), is the partial calva with facial fragments of a young adult male, a byrsoid brachymorph with sloping and pinched forehead, perceptible sagittal elevation, level elliptical orbits, and a light jaw with median chin and good dentition with slight wear and one caries. The skeleton is strikingly tall (181 cm.), though not rugged, with platymeria and eurycnemia.

N/3744 is the calvaria of a middle-aged male from Bogenšperk (Wagensberg) near Magdalenska gora. This is a low-headed ovoid brachycrane with narrow forehead, expansively rounded parietals and occiput, narrow and high nose root, and good teeth with medium wear. The skeleton indicates fairly tall stature, (174 cm.) massive bones, eurymeria, and koilorachic lumbar region.

N/3708 (Tumulus X, grave 16), is a young adult female calva, ovoid and with low forehead.

N/3709 (Tumulus X, grave 18), is a young adult female cranium, slightly warped, massive, ovoid, with well-filled temporals, pointed mastoids, and small lambdoid flattening. The low face has oblong orbits, concave nose with pinched root, shallow pointed chin, poor and markedly worn teeth and probably an edge bite (illustrated). This skull approaches closely Ofnet K 1802.

N/3732 (Tumulus IV, grave 14), is a young adult female calva, ovoid (-byrsoid), with slightly pinched forehead, and jaw with median chin.

Generalizing from these descriptions and from the average measurements listed in Tables I and II, I can describe the average Hallstatt Illyrian from Magdalenska gora as follows.

He is tall, with big and heavy bones without excessive muscular crests. The femora are just platymeric and have perceptible pilasters. Tibiae are eurycnemic.

There is only slight retroversion of the tibiae at the knee, and slight to medium femoral torsion below the hip, though flexion facets at the ankle are more often present than absent. The lumbar curve is probably not strong. Thus the supposed hallmarks of mountaineer's or athlete's gait and posture are not clearly developed. Three lumbar column average heights of 141.9 and 143 (ant. and post.) suggest a big trunk. Probably the body build was heavy, possibly somewhat corpulent, and certainly powerful.

The skull is also large and massive, mesocrane, with a notably well-filled ovoid-ellipsoid form, broad and blunt forehead on a big frontal bone somewhat pinched above the malar junction, and with medium to heavy browridges. The forehead, like the vault as a whole, is of medium height, but slopes only slightly. The short parietals show some sagittal thickening, not really scaphoid, with little curve interruption at lambda. The occiput is fully rounded with small to medium mound-shaped torus. Temporals are rounded but do not bulge and the long mastoids are medium-large in size. The capacious skull base has clearcut condyles, not depressed, a fairly steep articular eminence, and an oval-elliptical auditory meatus with somewhat thin tympanic plate. The face is large, with elongated hexagonal mean proportions and mesoprosopy. The large and high quadrilateral orbits tilt little, being ringed by laterally flaring cheekbones which retreat somewhat in profile. Nasion depression is not notable, the nose is mesorrhine, large, thick, fairly high at root and bridge and hence not salient, with straight (-wavy) profile and small nasal spine. Though the profile is orthognathous as a whole, some mouth prognathism occurs, most obviously in the mandible. The jaw is large and heavy, with obtuse-angled average jowls, and a deep triangular chin of small-medium protrusion. A capacious and fairly high palate is needed for the large teeth, of good quality, showing slightly more than medium wear mostly with an edge bite, slight crowding, and very few suppressed third molars. Few teeth are lost in life, but a few (1–4) caries is the rule. Abscesses are also rare, but tend to be large when they occur.

This average description differs from the Greek Mixed Alpine type in the bigger and higher face, orbits, and nose, relatively narrower frontal, and slightly larger and better filled vault of the Magdalenska gora group: divergences in both Nordic and to a lesser extent Alpine directions. And general consideration of the individual skull descriptions confirms the split between the high-headed, horse-faced dolicho-mesocrane Nordics in the group and the low-headed, big and round-faced brachycrane Alpines as the main source of racial interaction, without any smooth junction of these contrasting tendencies by Mixed Alpines or Dinarics, and with some added variety resulting from Basic White and Mediterranean influences. Hence it is clear that the people of Magdalenska gora formed a racially heterogeneous community. Subjectively this heterogeneity appears about equivalent to that of the beginning of the Iron Age in Greece, the population of Magdalenska gora appearing definitely less homogeneous than Classical Greeks (except possibly Macedonians) and less heterogeneous than Greeks of the Middle Bronze Age (Angel, 1960).

On the other hand, the groups are knit together by certain small similarities, possibly family traits, between skulls of contrasting type such as N/3711 and N/3719, N/3697 and N/3683, N/3699 and N/3712; note that the last two of these pairs are not from the same tumuli either. There are two sets of trait combinations which to a large extent crosscut the differences between types, showing the phaenotypic proof of recombinations (and presumably crossing over of linkage groups) to be expected in a normal mixing population. The first of these is the arched, slightly pinched, and incipiently byrsoid frontal bone, sometimes going with a high-arched nose, a combination seen in eight skulls, (N/3711, 3714, 3721, 3719, 3725, 3744, 3708, and 3732) and contrasting with a square, "box-like" frontal bone generally accompanying a blunt ovoid *norma verticalis*. The second is the combination of convex or slightly prognathous mouth

region with sloping teeth row and jaw with somewhat receding chin, tilted corpus, and relatively short ramus, which is especially noticeable in the Alpine group since it looks out of place there as also in Neolithic Cypriotes from Khirokitia (Angel, 1953), (N/3713, 3719, 3691, 3704, 3703, 3683, 3711, 3714, and 3716 in descending order of definiteness). We might expect strongly buttressed nasal bones, generally high-bridged, to accompany a tilted palate and chewing plane in skulls like these which have retreating, non-Mongoloid cheekbones: the chewing stresses from the first molars will tend to pass up more anteriorly toward the vault than in skulls with a horizontal chewing plane or a much greater use of anterior masseter and maxillary ridge.

These peculiarities, as well as the occurrence of unexpectedly high orbits, must be special local trait recombinations which the types used here are too crude to explain. All this makes the Magdalenska gora series appear as a relatively isolated group where the last extensive mixture took place three generations or so before the late Hallstatt period (i.e., during a period of cremation from which no data are obtainable), and when there was less immigration into Slovenia than must have occurred during Keltic, Imperial Roman, Gothic, Slavic, or Mediaeval German occupation.

There are 21 males and 11 females (including one notably arthritic skeleton) available for age estimation. On this basis the average age at death was 40.7 for males, and 31.3 for females. This is a big sex difference, perhaps partly from sampling accident, but is in the usual direction for ancient or mediaeval populations: women die young because of childbirth hazards and hard work. The Magdalenska gora population lived less long than Classical Greeks (44.5 males; 34.9 females) but longer than Early Iron Age Greeks (38.5 males; 30.7 females) who would be in part the close *cultural* ancestors of the Hallstatt period peoples accessible via the Adriatic Sea, and whose culture was roughly comparable in level.

COMPARISON

(1) The earliest of the groups chosen for comparison is that from the Mesolithic of Bavaria, remains of the presumed cult of decapitation (Scheidt, 1923, Gieseler, 1938). In addition to both massive (Borreby) and low-headed varieties of Alpine and Mixed Alpine,

the Bavarian series includes the somewhat mesocrane, low-orbitted, Mesolithic Mediterranean as at Téviec (Boule and Vallois, 1937) with its inclusion of "Cro-Magnon" or Basic White tendencies as in K 1818, and production of varying intermediate individuals.[8] The central tendency is therefore toward a large-vaulted mesocrane, high, ovoid, with sloping forehead and face less variable than the vault. This is a square, low, broad-jawed, deep-chinned face, with nondescript mesorrhine nose, strikingly low orbits, wide interorbital space, broad palate, and incipient prognathism.

(2) The East Balkan-Ukraine Neolithic-Chalcolithic group diverges from the slightly earlier Bavarian Mesolithic group in smaller vault and face size, slightly narrower vault and definitely narrower face. There is probable similarity in their low upper faces, mesorrhiny, low orbits, slight prognathism, and deep jaws: the "Mesolithic" elements in both series include Alpines and primitive Mediterraneans. Thus the east Balkan series shows parallelism in its Alpine and primitive Mediterranean blending. But here the "European" Alpines are less rugged and smaller; low-headed, sphenoid, low-faced, broad-nosed, and sometimes slightly prognathous Alpines compare just as well with one element in early Neolithic Cyprus (Angel, 1953) or the later low-headed Alpines of Asia Minor as with Ofnet, Furfooz, or Lake Ladoga low-headed, brachy-mesocranes (Krogman, 1937, Coon, 1939, p. 125, Angel, 1951). And Jaranov's prognathous, broad-nosed, small-skulled "Proto-mediterraneans" of N. Bulgaria could be connected with South Russia or Asia Minor (Coon, 1939, pp. 103–136), at the end of Mesolithic times, forming one element in Coon's Danubian type. Similarly the Basic White (Upper Palaeolithic) element can spring from this Russian source (Debetz, 1960). Hence the plausible "pre-Neolithic" elements in the eastern Balkans link as definitely with the east and southeast at a post-Mesolithic date as with the Bavarian Mesolithic group.

But the really striking divergence in the East Balkan series is the appearance of hawk-nosed, deep-vaulted, long-faced early Iranians or Nordics (Coon's Corded, Danubian and Cappadocian types) obviously of eastern derivation, since no northwestern source is available in the fourth or third millennia B.C. Mixture results in fully Dinaric-Mediterranean rather than Mixed Alpine forms, as also in the Macedonian Neolithic skulls from Servia and Nea Nikomedeia.

(3) The early Yugoslavian crania, from Ig just south of Ljubljana, are not much earlier than the late Hallstatt series from Slovenia and may be later than these.[9] They are all of dominantly Basic White type, rugged, with sloping and pinched foreheads, deep occiputs, and both scaphoid and filled-out parietal tendencies. They show incipient Mixed Alpine fullness. And they would derive either from Bavarian Mesolithic or more plausibly from some southern Adriatic population such as that of Submycenaean Cephallenia (Angel, 1943). The Ig skulls would fit perfectly into the Magdalenska gora series.

(4) Magdalenska gora is surprisingly similar to the Bavarian Mesolithic averages shown in Table IV, differing only in a more pinched forehead, more orthognathous and much higher and more hexagonal face, strikingly higher orbits, and bigger nose. The Alpine and part of the Mediterranean elements in the Magdalenska gora group are certainly of Bavarian Mesolithic descent. But these Illyrians diverge from the latter in showing a potent minority of Corded Nordics, together with a tendency to form Dinaric-Mediterranean hybrid types (as well as the more numerous Mixed Alpines). Thus in these respects the people of Magdalenska gora paralleled the East Balkan divergence from the Bavarian Mesolithic group. And a comparison of the Slovenian Nordic element with Hallstatt Illyrian series from Austria shows obvious connection as seen in Table IV.

Pontic Mediterranean influence may have reached Slovenia from the east likewise. But the similarity of such crania as N/3686 and N/3726 as well as the Ig skulls to Basic Whites from the Ionian Islands (Cephallenia) is probably more important.

---

[8] As in Kaufertsberg and Hohlenstein Bavarians. Compare also the Montardit Mixed Alpine (R. S. Wallis, 1931) and the Nagy Sap Dinaric (F. von Luschan, 1872). The part played by Neolithic intruders in these mixtures is hard to evaluate without more archaeological evidence for dating.

[9] No N. Yugoslavian crania intervene between these and Krapina Neanderthal series.

Comparison of Magdalenska gora with Classical Greece stresses the greater massiveness, broader and fuller vaults, larger and more hexagonal faces, bigger noses, higher orbits, greater mouth protrusion, and more obtuse jaw angles of the Illyrians. This emphasizes their much stronger Alpine–Mixed Alpine and weaker Mediterranean tendencies as well as superiority in gross body size. And it lends point to the similarity of individual Chalcidian Alpine–Mixed Alpine crania to Illyrians of Slovenia (Angel, 1942, p. 219).

Vram's "ancient" Slovenian crania of various dates[10] give a series which centers on the third or fourth century A.D., covering the range from 500 B.C. to 1000 A.D. at latest. Though the five late Hallstatt skulls from Vače (Watsch) would fit perfectly with the Alpine, Dinaric-Mediterranean, and Mediterranean elements from Magdalenska gora (lacking Nordic), Vram's "ancient" series as a whole shows less Alpine and massive Alpine and more Dinaric and small-skulled Nordic (and Pontic Mediterranean?) than do the Illyrians of Magdalenska gora. On the whole the very striking decrease in gross size which Vram's dominantly Roman period series shows for Illyrians of Slovenia seems more important than slight changes in proportions seen in narrower vault and jowls and broader nose. The size decrease parallels that between Central European Hallstatt (largely Nordic) and La Tène (smaller and more Dinaric-Alpine) groups (Coon, 1939), and between Greek Classical and Roman period groups (Angel, 1951, 1960).

Vram's series is also much closer to the Bosnian Illyrians of Hallstatt through Roman date from the Glasinac plateau tumuli than are the latter to Magdalenska gora. The Glasinac series (Weisbach, 1897, 1907; Schwidetz-

ky, 1940) seems to have less marked Nordic and stronger Alpine, small Dinaric, and Mixed Alpine elements than the Slovenia group.

(5) Vram's mediaeval group from Ljubljana show a still stronger contrast to the Magdalenska gora series in the direction foreshadowed by the Glasinac series. These mediaeval Slovenes are medium-sized, low-vaulted, short-based brachycranes, with pinched foreheads, ovoid-sphenoid vaults, and medium-large, strong-jowled and deep-jawed (?) faces marked out more by very high orbits than by low mesorrhine noses. They consist almost wholly of Alpines and true Dinarics with a minority of Mixed Alpines. And they compare very closely with modern Carinthians as well as with modern Slovenes. The mediaeval Slovenes differ from modern Carinthians of partly Slovene origin only in their slightly narrower faces and much higher orbits. On the other hand the modern Slovenes of Weisbach (1912; Morant, 1928) have higher and more brachycrane vaults, bigger faces, and lower orbits than their mediaeval ancestors. The original Slavic population of the Drave valley (Ivaniček, 1951), however, contrasts very strongly with the modern Carinthian population in the direction of the Hallstatt-La Tène population: more Iron Age Nordic and Mixed Alpine, with the same massiveness seen in the Magdalenska gora group 14 centuries earlier. Apparently in Carinthia the change in an Alpine direction was later and more sudden than in Slovenia or Bosnia, and could represent a northern intrusion from this southern Slav center of short-headedness.

These contrasts stress the fact that it is much easier to find continuity between Bavarian Mesolithic and E. Balkan Chalcolithic series and Magdalenska gora Illyrians than between the latter and mediaeval or modern South Slavs. The only modern group comparable to the Magdalenska gora series are the Old Montenegrins described by Coon, (1939, pp. 591–595) quoting data of R. Ehrich. But it is paradoxically easy to show simple Alpine continuity between Mesolithic and Modern.

---

[10] Vače (Watsch) in north central Slovenia (Hallstatt), Slepsech and Gorianchi (Keltic-Roman?), Ljubljana (Imperial Roman), Dernovo in E. Slovenia (Roman), Veldes in N. W. Slovenia (early Slavic), and Heiligenberg in N. C. Slovenia (early Slavic with Merovingian influence).

DISCUSSION

Although Slovenia was a marginal area until an Iron Age peddling and mining economy exploited it, it has provided no real evidence

for survival of any genes derived from the Krapina subtype of Neanderthal. It is true that the people of Magdalenska gora show many traits which could have such an origin; for instance, massiveness, broad and low vaults of Alpine group, with short brain-space; large orbits; large teeth, and linked mouth features. Allowing for the enormous complexity of inheritance of skull form, for some process of infantilization, and for the principles of relative growth, it is not unreasonable to derive Alpines as a whole from Neanderthal mixture with other forms of man in Europe (F. Weidenreich, 1941; C. S. Coon, 1939, pp. 38–39, p. 119). But evidence is insufficient.

It seems most probable that an Alpine–Mixed Alpine population, with slight crude Mediterranean influence (like the Bavarian Mesolithic) inhabited the Chalcolithic pile-dwelling settlement of the Ljubljana moor (Ig) from the late third millennium B.C. onward. Danubian and Corded Nordic invaders suggested by Bodrogkeresztur metallurgical influence before and Corded ceramic influence after 2000 B.C. may have had slight effect. Cypriot and Aegean ceramic influence claimed perceptible in Slavonian pottery suggests some possible effects of the Adriatic–Central European trade route on the mountain-isolated pre-Indo-European population of Slovenia (C.F.C. Hawkes, 1940, pp. 246–49). Since this was the route by which Iron Age economy finally reached Slovenia it almost undoubtedly accounts for the Basic White and some of the Mediterranean elements in the Magdalenska gora series. The Nordic minority at Magdalenska gora with equal probability penetrated Slovenia somewhat earlier (with Hungarian urnfields and Lausitz influence?) from east and northeast. Presumably this intrusion brought in Illyrian speech.

With increasing Italic influence and the La Téne Keltic penetration of Slovenia small-vaulted Nordics and Mediterraneans challenge Alpine predominance, though the size reduction which is the chief biological change in imperial Roman times may have some selective or environmental explanation. The Ostrogoths, Merovingians, and presumably also the first Slav-speakers reaching Slovenia brought a Nordic blend with Mixed Alpines and Dinarics resulting from mixture with the persistent Alpines, perhaps like the Carinthian Slavic sample. It is conceivable that a very late post-Slavic southward movement did bring in still more Alpines, since the movement southward of the Slovenes was not fully completed into Slovenia until they were incorporated into the Holy Roman Empire as part of the Ostmark, and Germanic-speaking Alpine peasants pushed into them. Drave valley Slavs were not alpinized until *after* the 10th century A.D. In general the progressive alpinization of mediaeval Slovenia or Carinthia, like that of Bavaria, must result from multiplication of Mesolithic elements traceable through the Iron Age of Slovenia more clearly than that of Bavaria. And, on the other hand, the Dinaric type's salience in Slovenia must represent facial traits of Hallstatt Nordics.

CONCLUSIONS

(1) Magdalenska gora Illyrians were an heterogeneous group, including: massive Alpines (31%) of eventual Palaeolithic descent; both rugged (10%) and gracile (10%) Mediterraneans partly of Mesolithic descent and partly of Aegean-Adriatic origin; high-headed Nordics (17%) of eastern origin whose Late Bronze Age (?) invasion introduced Illyrian speech; and massive Mixed Alpine (28%–) and Dinaric–Mediterranean (4%–) hybrids not smoothly fusing the group.

(2) Mixture between these was leading toward some group unity seen in similar detail complexes in skulls of contrasting type. Slovenia probably retained much of its prehistoric isolation down to Imperial Roman exploitation of Illyricum.

(3) Magdalenska gora compares well with no later SE. European group except perhaps Old Montenegrins.

(4) Full Dinarics do not seem important until Roman times.

(5) Many further inferences are possible. For instance, the continuity between Mesolithic and Mediaeval Alpines is again confirmed. Approximation of the Bronze Age population of Slovenia allows more accurate guesses concerning the origin of Dorians and perhaps also of Macedonians.